THE DYING CHILD

THE DYING CHILD

Jo-Eileen Gyulay, R.N., M.S.
Formerly Instructor, Department of Pediatrics
School of Medicine
University of Kansas Medical Center

McGraw-Hill Book Company
A Blakiston Publication
New York   St. Louis   San Francisco   Auckland
Bogotá   Düsseldorf   Johannesburg   London   Madrid
Mexico   Montreal   New Delhi   Panama   Paris
São Paulo   Singapore   Sydney   Tokyo   Toronto

NOTICE

Medicine is an ever-changing science. As new research and clinical experience broaden our knowledge, changes in treatment and drug therapy are required. The editors and the publisher of this work have made every effort to ensure that the drug dosage schedules herein are accurate and in accord with the standards accepted at the time of publication. Readers are advised, however, to check the product information sheet included in the package of each drug they plan to administer to be certain that changes have not been made in the recommended dose or in the contraindications for administration. This recommendation is of particular importance in regard to new or infrequently used drugs.

THE DYING CHILD

1 2 3 4 5 6 7 8 9 0   DODO   7 8 3 2 1 0 9 8 7

This book was set in Press Roman by Allen Wayne Technical Corp. The editor was Mary Ann Richter; the cover was designed by Albert M. Cetta; the production supervisor was Jeanne Selzam.
R. R. Donnelley & Sons Company was printer and binder.

Library of Congress Cataloging in Publication Data

Gyulay, Jo-Eileen.
    The dying child.

    "A Blakiston publication."
    Bibliography: p.
    Includes index.
    1. Terminally ill children. 2. Pediatric
nursing. I. Title.
RJ47.5.G97   362.7'8   77-11655
ISBN 0-07-025360-9

To each of the children and their families mentioned anonymously in this text for allowing me the privilege of sharing in the care of their treasured, short lives

I Love You!

To my Father and Mother who in giving me life allowed me to share love.

Thank You!

Contents

Preface

Two generations ago death was a fact of life. People died at home surrounded by those they loved. Children joined their parents in caring for the dying, and participated in the rituals of death. In those days, the death of a child was not an infrequent occurrence. Parents accepted the possibility of losing one or more of their children. Today, because of modern equipment and advanced technology, many diseases that were formerly devastating killers have been controlled or eradicated. Sophisticated diagnostic techniques, immunization, surgery, chemotherapy, transplantation, and radiotherapy all contribute to the cure or containment of disease. Nevertheless, the fears and anxieties surrounding death appear to have increased, even though the projected life expectancy is now over 70 years. Palliative treatment can prolong survival in the hope of possible new therapy or cure. Ironically, as a result of the protectiveness, our attitudes often deny us our humanness and strip us of our basic rights to discuss, explore, and share our feelings.

All too often, American society deals with death by denying it. Serious discussion is suppressed because it arouses intense emotion and makes people feel uncomfortable. At the same time, America incessantly glorifies the deaths of fictional characters and of anonymous victims of crime and war. One can hardly pick up a newspaper or turn on a television set without seeing a dramatic depiction of death. Americans seem to be fascinated by the spectacle of violence and war, but unwilling to confront the reality of death in their daily lives.

In recent years, however, both professional and laypersons have begun to explore the subject of death more seriously. Seminars, church-sponsored symposiums, college and high school courses, radio and television shows have all undertaken to discuss the many aspects of the grief process, death, and dying. The response has been tremendous. The desire for more knowledge about death and dying has been overwhelming.

The purpose of this book is to examine death as another facet of the *life* experience. It has occurred to this author that the subject of death and dying may simply connote finality and hopelessness. Anyone who makes this assumption from reading the title misses the basic fact that death is a life experience. We all have to face death as does the child whose life is shortened by fatal illness, congenital anomalies, or irreversible injuries.

Each one of us is dying, but it is how we live that affects the termination of life, either our own or the life of those we care for. Until one explores one's own philosophy of life and death, one cannot effectively help others. Helping others cope with death does not mean forcing our own philosophy on them. We must first examine our concepts and begin to free ourselves of the hang-ups, fears, misconceptions, and rationalizations that define death for us. Only then will we be able to sympathize with and care for those who are grieving their own impending death or that of a loved one.

Each child is a unique individual, but he is also a sociological force in the family and the community, in school, and in the hospital. His life, brief though it is, touches the lives of many people. Every relationship implies reciprocity, and the nurse must share in the life of the dying child if she is to give him the best possible care. Sharing means listening to the child and his family, growing with them, being involved in their experiences, both painful and pleasant, and trying to understand exactly what the child and his loved ones are expressing.

The purpose of this book is to focus on children who are dying, children whose lives have been shortened by incurable illness, congenital anomalies, sudden, unexpected death, or irreversible injuries. The book is written from the point of view and based on the experiences of a pediatric nurse, but is applicable to all members of the health care team.

The author has been privileged to share the experiences of the children, families, and others anonymously described in this text. In this sense, this book has not been written by one person but by many — the children, their loved ones, and the fellow staff members who have been the real teachers of the meaning of life and death: pain, joy, grief, frustration, puzzlement, hopelessness, and hope.

ACKNOWLEDGMENTS

To Frank Barhydt, Sally Barhydt, Irene Gunther, and Mary Ann Richter, editors whose support and patience with my manuscript has been limitless.

To Martha Barnard, whose inspiration and encouragement allowed me to begin writing.

To Jan Black, whose precious fingers typed the manuscript.

To Edward Christopherson, Ph.D., whose encouragement and energy made me finish the tasks at hand.

To Drs. Nathan Goldstein and Rolf Habersang, whose support and understanding have been limitless during the difficult time of writing this text.

To Bonnie Hedin and Lisa Simkins, who spent endless hours helping with the bibliography.

To Lois Hedin, who has been a neighbor in every aspect of the term.

To Dr. Elisabeth Kübler-Ross, whose encouragement and support allowed me to share my love for the terminally ill.

To Dr. James Lowman, who helped me begin the work with terminally ill children.

To Ruth and Bill Moore, who provided unlimited support, editing, friendship, and coffee during the long months of writing.

To Sean Mulloy and Emmanuel Thomas, whose friendship and support have been treasured.

To Suzanne Shaffer, a colleague whose support and friendship have been deeply appreciated.

To Kerry Lynn Sullivan, my niece, who spent many hours helping with the manuscript.

Without these persons, and many relatives and friends, this book could not have been written. I deeply appreciate your support and encouragement.

Jo-Eileen Gyulay

Reactions to Grief

From the time of diagnosis until the death itself both the family and the child go through a progression of psychological adjustments in order to accept the fatal outcome. The reactions to grief listed below do not describe the behavior of all parents or all children, and not everyone experiences each and every reaction. Frequently the reactions shift back and forth with the fluctuations in the course of the illness, that is, remission, exacerbations, and complications. The uncertainties of the outcome or even of the child's condition may mean that parent and child are at different stages at a given time.

The identification of five stages of grief[1] by Elisabeth Kübler-Ross, from denial of death through rage, bargaining, depression and finally acceptance, is, with a few additions, the basis for the list that follows.

Guilt: Intense feelings of having possibly done something wrong either by commission, omission, thought, or action. Guilt usually begins either in the pre-

---

[1] Elisabeth Kübler-Ross, *On Death and Dying*, Macmillan, New York, 1969, Chaps. 3–7.

diagnostic period or at the time of sudden unexpected death. It often intensifies periodically throughout the course of the illness and postdeath period.

Shock: The numbness and "unreal" feeling that begins at the time of diagnosis, or perhaps even before, when there is a threat of serious diagnosis. It can last for days or weeks after the diagnosis. Typically the feelings may reoccur at stressful times during the course of the illness and after death.

Denial: The disbelief that often occurs at the same time as or immediately following the shock stage. Denial may or may not be verbalized. The louder the verbalization, and the more strident the protests, the closer one is to realizing the truth. The stage is best expressed by: "This can't be happening to me (patient) or to us (parents, others)!" Denial may be present throughout the course of the illness and postdeath period, but usually it is episodic in nature. Extended denial with unrealistic behavior may be indicative of pathology.

Somatic complaints: Whirling or pounding in the head, gastric distress such as indigestion, nausea, vomiting, diarrhea, constipation, heaviness or crushing feeling in the chest, pounding heart, lump in the throat, tingling, numbness, menstrual irregularities, sighing, shortness of breath, fatigue, anorexia or increased appetite, restlessness, insomnia, or nightmares. Family members often fear they also will die when they are suffering from somatic distress.

Anger: "It's not fair!" Hostile conduct, verbalization, passive, or aggressive behavior that may be directed to those emotionally close to the grieving persons, to casual acquaintances, or to total strangers. Periodic outbursts may cause severe distress with relationships, embarrassment, guilt, and withdrawal.

Fears: Realistic, or unfounded by personal experiences or those of others. Sensations described vary from nagging indescribable uneasiness to gripping panic. Fear may lead one to believe that one is losing one's mind or cause chronic anxieties about the uncertain, painful future.

Bargaining: "If . . . maybe . . . possibly . . . please!" This is the stage in which grieving persons make conscious or unconscious promises or attempt to strike bargains with God, themselves, health care providers, institutions or others to change the situation either permanently or at least until a cure can be obtained. Some promises made or measures taken may be quite unrealistic, for instance, hoping the child will regain health in exchange for the parent becoming a "perfect" parent, or discontinuing various attitudes or behaviors (e.g., drinking, an affair, lack of faith).

Awareness of the reality of the situation: Realizing the inevitability of the impending death. Denial defenses, bargaining, and anger have not taken the illness away. The end seems inescapable.

Depression: When bargaining, denial, and other defenses have failed and awareness of the inevitable death grows, anger is vented inwardly and depression follows. It is usually manifested by withdrawal, detachment, nonverbalization, crying, or inability to concentrate except on the impending death. Other symptoms are feelings of worthlessness, occasional suicidal thoughts, and constant fatigue accompanied by the inability to rest or sleep. The grieving person usually chooses one or a few significant persons with whom to share his or her feelings.

Reestablishment of emotional attachment to others: This may take place at any time during the course of the anticipatory grief or years after the death. The impending loss is recognized and other relationships (with spouse, siblings, family, friends, other patients) are again seen as desirable, worthwhile, or at least tolerable.

Acceptance of the loss: Not all grieving people reach this stage. "It (death) has taken place, but I can't do anything about it. He (she) will not live (or come back)." Many find peace in this stage, even elation that they have worked through the process of grief. This stage is often, though not always, arrived at through religious beliefs. It is not necessarily permanent, nor the last stage in grief. The grieving person may have slipped back into an earlier reaction, resignation, which is not to be confused with acceptance. On the contrary, resignation brings with it intense anger and hostility.

Return to a normal active life with the loss a part of that life: This normal life may not be the normal life experienced before the loss. Being active in this stage differs from the restlessness that occurs in the anger and depression stages. It implies the resumption of a useful and meaningful way of life. The death is not forgotten, and will always be a part of the grieving person; however, in time the constant preoccupation with the dead person will fade. In its place, will come happier memories and reorganization of life without the deceased. Not all grieving persons achieve this.

Part One

The Child

Chapter 1

Young Children

I look at these children and see an aging that I can't describe. You have to look in their eyes. There is a maturity that only an experience like this can give. They may still act like children but they are different.

I'll miss you, too, Mom, but I'm ready.

The responsibility for caring for a healthy, normal child is a challenging one; but for the parents of a child with a fatal illness, congenital anomalies, or irreversible injuries the demands can be unrelenting. The child's understanding and acceptance of the situation will depend upon a number of factors including his maturity, his background, and his capabilities, but the primary factor is the attitude of his parents.

From the time of diagnosis, a child's life changes radically. A secure world ceases to exist and in its place comes a new environment filled with procedures, lab results, radiological reports, and medications. Suddenly, life centers on the disease. The child's developmental milestones and personal needs are often forgotten in the process of giving the physical care needed to sustain even limited life expectancy. The health care providers may become so involved in lifesaving measures, protocols, research, and education that the individuality of the child and family is lost in the shuffle. Plans, assessments, and goals may not take account of her uniqueness, for example, her age and family responsibilities, her relationship with siblings, the size of the family and how much attention she gets, and whether she is the oldest, middle, or youngest child.

Although children may not understand either the diagnosis, the prognosis, or the therapy, they are adept at reading messages, and picking up cues and signals from those around them. They quickly recognize that something bad is happening to them and to those around them. Children perceive what is happening on a feeling level: mother, father, sister, brother, relatives, friends and possibly even the staff appear to be afraid both of them and for them. Their parents are suddenly protective to the point of smothering. Regression, temper tantrums, or various other forms of misbehavior may all of a sudden not only be allowed, but even encouraged.

Even the very young child senses tension. When the family receives bad news (e.g., negative prognosis, relapse, the need for new therapy, complications, etc.) the parents' emotional reaction is understood by the child. Staff members have observed infants as young as 8 months, as well as retarded children, whose behavior changed following the word of impending tragedy. A child who moments before had been vying for the attention of his parents became quiet and sat motionless on the parent's lap as if fully understanding the impact of the news. One young girl appropriately wiped tears from her mother's cheeks with the poise of an adult.

The phenomenon of role reversal that occurs at times of stress and crisis, and in which children become the main source of comfort and support for the parents, is common in older children, but occasionally has been observed among children as young as 3. Their reassurances, "Don't worry," "It's not your fault," "It doesn't hurt much," "I'll be brave," typically are followed by a patient acceptance of procedures that were previously marked by loud protests. Tad, age 3, went over to his mother after she had comforted him during several unsuccessful venipunctures. She had given him considerable support throughout the painful, frustrating ordeal, and Tad had cried frequently during the long process. She, too, began to cry since they had to face still more attempts. He gave her a hug and a kiss, patted her on the leg, and said, "It's okay. I'm okay, Mommy, I love you."

The preschooler seeks comfort, reassurance, and support from her parents. They are her main protectors, and when they fail she regards this as a transgression of catastrophic proportions. Her protectors appear to be granting permission for the indignities and pain she is subjected to. From her standpoint, the wall of protection, security, and love is crumbling, a terrifying feeling. As yet, the preschooler is unable to grasp the impact of her illness or injuries because her primary concern is the change she sees in those around her.

Children often blame parents for causing and allowing pain. This can be acutely disturbing to parents because so often they, too, believe they are responsible. The child's assertions seem correct: Through some negligence on their part the disease was allowed to spring up in the first place. Usually the young child's outbursts increase the parents' sense of guilt and create mixed feelings toward the therapy. Even when parents participate in the care of their children, a child screaming, "I hate you," "You don't care," "You don't do anything," or "Why won't you help me?" has a devastating effect. Following such an outburst, it is not uncommon for parents and child to withdraw from each other, feeling guilty and embarrassed. However, any attempt to reassure the young child that his parents are doing everything they can to help him may result in another tirade of anger or else complete silence. The child may literally turn his back on his parents or, to further dramatize his displeasure, refuse to eat or drink, bathe, take medications, or cooperate in any way with parents or staff. He may yell that he wishes his mother or father dead. He does not know what this means, but he knows the word "death" makes everyone extremely uncomfortable. Under the circumstances, such a taunt may produce an emotional reaction that makes the young child feel guilty for having uttered it. He is then overwhelmed by guilt, feeling he deserves the awful things that are happening to him. The reassurances of family do not remove all his doubts because he sees the staff and their equipment as a constant threat. They are like monsters ready to steal him from his security and comfort.

A 4-year-old boy whose mother was not able to be at the hospital constantly because of heavy family responsibilities would scream angrily over the telephone at her, "I don't like you. I don't want you to come." After his outburst a period of silence would follow. The distressed mother would explain how much she loved and missed him. The child offered no response. After hanging up, however, he would cry, "Will mommy be here when I have my shot?"

People unconsciously give the child cues that tell him how to manipulate the staff and his parents. He knows what makes parents feel guilt. The child may play one relationship against another (e.g., parent against parent, parent against sibling, sibling against sibling, relative against parent, etc.). The 3-year-old child is able to assess individual weaknesses, and he uses the manipulative behavior most effective against each person, whether it be withdrawal, laughter, sweetness, bravery, stoicism, dependency, independence, or foul language. Younger children are not so adept. They may employ the same threat for each person they encounter: "I'll tell my Mommy on you!"

Out of momentary frustration or to manipulate his surroundings, the child may set limits on his participation in play activities. He may refuse to attend certain functions or publicly vow not to participate in social activities. Getting him back into the activities may require the assistance of staff. After attending a gathering that looks like one he might enjoy, he finds himself caught between standing firm on principle or joining in the fun. Some children do better if their protests are ignored, while others may need a plausible excuse before they can comfortably rejoin a group.

Usually the extent to which the child tries to manipulate people depends on how miserable he is as well as on the insecurities, guilt, and the stage of grief being experienced by his victims. The chance to be daring or to behave in ways that would have been considered unacceptable prior to diagnosis is often appealing to him. The chance to control also offers gratification, but the child soon becomes afraid because his security is stripped away. He realizes that the misbehavior that once brought punishment now brings a love pat and a smile, and this inconsistency creates insecurity. The preschooler thrives on consistency and routine, and would prefer the old regimen with discipline. For instance, he may probe, "Why do you let me do this?" or, "Are you sure I can do that?" He may be too frightened to verbalize but simply retreat and become moody when every one gives in to him. A fatally sick child endures constant interruptions of his life through hospitalization and the inherent problems of the disease, all of which bring added insecurity. He is often spoiled by everyone, including staff. No matter how strong the family, discipline is difficult, and remains a constant problem throughout the course of illness.

THE OPEN SETTING

In lieu of straightforward answers about what is happening to her, a child often has to rely on her own guesswork and fantasies. In an open setting, the child is given answers that are intelligible to her and not discouraged from asking questions. The success of the open setting largely depends on the cooperation of the hospital staff and their ability to provide a model for the family to follow. The staff's poise, skill in providing appropriate answers to questions, and ability to help the family deal with unfamiliar situations are key ingredients for the success of the open setting.

In general, if the family has not been open in dealing with the child before the diagnosis, it is unlikely that their approach will change spontaneously afterwards. Yet even parents who were not in the habit of dealing with their children in a straightforward manner find it difficult to continue sheltering the child after the diagnosis. From the child's standpoint, an increase in the number of presents he receives, frequent surprises and favors, and a sudden curtailment of discipline make him more insecure than he would be if his parents told him truthfully that things were destined to be unpleasant. His most immediate fear is not of leukemia but of somehow being the source of everyone's discomfort. The child begins to realize that everything is being said or done to him and around him, and that he is not a participant in his own life.

The young child communicates primarily, perhaps even exclusively, with his parents. When this communication is cut off because the parents do not know how to deal with the situation, the child feels completely isolated. In his isolation he is as much a stranger to his parents as they are to him. The child's only understanding of what is happening to him comes from what he is told. The child can only become aware of the disease process and the effects it will have on his life if this is explained to him by his parents.

A child will often reiterate what the parents say, for example, "The doctors are doing these things not to hurt me but to make me feel better," "God lets me suffer because he loves me," or "Sickness brings families together." These statements have little meaning for a preschooler, but they are messages the parents either believe themselves or feel they should give to the child. By repeating these apothegms, the child demonstrates the extent to which he clings to his parents' words.

Because the young child believes that others can read his thoughts, he feels guilty when he thinks "bad" thoughts. He believes that anything he thinks, either good or bad, can come true. He is fearful of whatever else will happen to him because of his misbehavior, and often phrases this notion in the form of a bargain during painful and stressful procedures: "I promise I'll be good. I'm sorry, I won't do it again." All the painful experiences and all his misery, he feels, are punishment for his misdeeds. He does not realize that he can think good thoughts and bad thoughts without others knowing them. To remove these fears, the child needs reassurances from his family that they do not want him to be sick and in pain. Such reassurances do not settle his doubts entirely, but they do help the child endure painful procedures.

The more security and acceptance the child is given, the more he will be able to express his feelings — particularly his anger. The latter can be channeled and released in many ways, for example, by supplying the child with water, clay, a pounding board, the security of a stuffed animal, a bottle, or toys that suggest the security of his home. The important objective is to allow the child to express his true feelings. Often a child finds it easier and less threatening to talk to and through a "third person" such as a stuffed animal, a book, a toy, or other object than directly to an adult. One child revealed his fears when talking through his clown slippers. A staff member discovered this when she asked if the slippers, Herman and Harry, ever became afraid of being in the hospital. The child expressed his fears of shots and other pain, restraints, and separation from his mother. Through the clowns he conveyed his suspicion that a long illness meant that he was bad. At the end of the conversation, the staff member hugged both the slippers and the child. Immediately the child said, "I feel better. I was so scared." He cried for a short time in her arms then began to play. After several such sessions the child's anxieties decreased. Finally the staff member and the child talked less through Herman and Harry, and directly to one another.

Long descriptions and explanations are irritating to very young children. Only concise answers to their questions are appropriate. If they ask the same question several times, they are not only groping for meaning but also probing the consistency of the answers. An inappropriate or incomplete answer may activate the child's innate fears. The young child wants answers to her questions when she asks. A 4-year-old child may calmly ask about a fellow patient who died of the same disease she has while the rest of the family eats dinner. Overhearing others talk about the death of a fellow patient, she may ask what dying means, or what will happen to her if she does not get well. A convenient, evasive answer may satisfy her for a time, but eventually she may wonder, "Does God really love me if all the people He loves die?" Moreover, while being assured that God is good, heaven is a wonderful place to be, and no suffering is a blessing, she is quick to spot the fears and sadness in others when she asks about her own death.

The child who is allowed to see the true emotions of his parents rather than relying on his own intuition that something serious, yet unspoken, is happening to the family is better able to cope. Surrounded by honesty, even when the honesty is painful, he knows that he is part of the family and that he is trusted. In turn he trusts those around him when he feels free to ask and repeat questions about the things he does not understand.

An extremely resistant 5-year-old boy facing another in an endless series of spinal taps was told by the resident, "You needn't cry since your back is weeping for you." The resident then held up a tube of spinal fluid as if it were tacit proof of what he said. After the resident left, the child asked his mother what "weeping" meant. "Isn't that the dumbest thing?" the child said after hearing the answer. "It still takes a needle and somebody holding me like a frog. It hurts. That was spinal fluid he was holding up. Who does he think I am?"

The very young child needs his parents. Their presence provides security. He fears separation, abandonment, and pain, but not death. Time has no meaning to a child except as it pertains to his needs. His mother's absence during her lunch break seems an eternity to him, while time seems to fly when he is enjoying himself. When the child is told, "You'll go home next Wednesday," or "Your spinal tap won't be for two more weeks," he has little concept of the period of time involved, and this may be disturbing to him. Therefore a judgment should be made as to how far in advance a child should be told about a particular procedure, or about plans for his dismissal. Frequently children are unable to sleep when they know that the next afternoon a new test, or their dismissal, is scheduled. Anticipation is difficult even when the event is a happy one—everyone can remember when Christmas Eve was the longest night of the year. Even with assurance that "it won't be so bad," the child looks beyond the words at his mother's tension and anxiety. He cannot be fooled or cajoled into believing it will be that easy. An alert preschooler's response to such a statement might be, "Then you have it." Above all the child needs support in the face of stress, and the reassurance of his parents that they love him and will be with him.

PAIN AND SEPARATION

The greatest fears of the young child are of separation from mother (or mother figure) and of pain. But the emotional pain of parental separation is far greater than any physical pain the child has to endure. The parent is the support and strength of the child. He can never understand why his parents allow the assaults on him that stem from his illness, yet no one but they can provide the support, love, and concern he needs to endure these assaults. It is terrifying to the child to be denied this support system.

The toddler is unable to cope without his mother because he is incapable of making sense of what is going on. Others close to him—his father, a grandparent, a sibling—can substitute for the mother in her absence, but the toddler needs the security of a familiar face when hospital personnel are doing strange, painful, or restricting things to him. An infant of 4 or 5 months is aware of who is and who is not his mother, and he is quick to learn that the people who are not may do things to him that he is not going to like. During the course of illness, neither infant nor toddler may be comfortable with the staff; therefore, without the presence of a mother or mother figure, care may become much more complicated, and result in much more trauma.

HOSPITALIZATION IS NOT ALWAYS UNPLEASANT

There are times when children do not mind hospitalization. This is usually the case when the child is able to participate in fun activities such as play and occupational therapy, when fellow patients are present, restraints and procedures are at a minimum, and hospitalization is not an immediate threat to all concerned. It may be a time when the child has the undivided attention of parents, relatives, friends, and staff. He may be allowed to do what he wants, eat what he wants, participate in enjoyable activities, wheel around the halls at all hours of day or night, and wheedle surprises from parents and others.

When a child is desperately ill he usually does not object to an admission. He realizes that the hospital is the place where he will get help: "Mommy, why don't you call Dr. Jones? I think he can make me feel better." When a child is terminal and is aware of the helplessness of his family and their fear of having him at home, he may request hospitalization. Often the child comes to a point where he, too, may be afraid to be away from the hospital: "Everytime I go home my nose bleeds, my temperature goes up, I hurt. I'd rather stay here. They'll help us to make it feel better." As the child enters the terminal phase, particularly the terminal period, he often loses interest in the outside world. He is not interested in what is going on at home or in the community. He may become more depressed with each dismissal, having accepted the painful reality that he can no longer participate in and enjoy the activities of family and freinds. He may be pushed around more at home by siblings, or his care may be fragmented because people outside the hospital are unfamiliar with his needs. A 5-year-old told his mother one morning after he had been vomiting through the night (just secondary to intracranial pressure), "I think I better get back to the hospital. I need a spinal tap."

When the child is in the terminal period of her illness, she often, and quite deliberately, will cease talking about dismissal, return to school, beginning kindergarten, or any future plans. The child may become depressed or withdrawn. Many children will talk about death when allowed. They may ask, "What happens when people die?" or "What is Jesus' house like?" or talk about not having to be sick anymore, or wanting to see a relative or friend who preceded them in death. In some cases, a preschooler talks about his aspirations in the past tense: "When I wanted to be a fireman, a doctor, go to school . . . ." In such instances, children have a perfect understanding of tenses.

A child's concept of death matures as he does. Children under the age of 5 have difficulty with the concept: to them, death seems reversible. The preschooler may ask repeatedly if he is going to die. A simple yes or no may be all he wants, except for finding out whether it will hurt. An appropriate answer reduces the child's anxieties: "Yes, we are all going to die. Death makes us sad, but we will be with you so it won't hurt." Later the parents may reassure the child that when he has pain they will help make it hurt less. This is an honest approach, since death itself is not painful. In dealing with the child's questions, parents and staff will find that it helps the child if they separate pain from death.

Chapter 2

Older Children

I get so sick of them arguing whether I'm protocol number 6974 or 6942 or whatever. They don't even call me by name. I'm not human. I'm a number. They don't look at me. They look through me. Oh, never mind. They've got to do their thing. I'm just one of many, but I'm the only one I've got.

Between the ages of 6 and 12 a child grows emotionally and intellectually toward independence. The security of parents and home is no longer enough. Assurances that he is important must come from a wider assortment of people: peers, teachers, members of his community, and so on. If a single characteristic could be said to dominate the thinking of the school-age child and the adolescent, it would be the fear of being judged different: being different may lead to ridicule and rejection. The fears of the younger children are primarily projections from the parents or the family. Older children, however, receive constant feedback about themselves and their relationships from extensive contact with the outside world. The more they are involved in new and unfamiliar situations, the more fearful they tend to be. They are, or think they are, well aware of how the world assesses them. As long as the assessment is positive, and they are accepted, all is well.

The school-age child who is diagnosed as having a terminal illness deserves and needs to know all about that illness in order to cope with it emotionally as well as to participate in his own care. What he *is* told as much as what he is *not* told can determine how fully he lives his limited life.

Diagnosis of fatal illness is a traumatic experience for the young child. However, this is usually because the parents' reaction makes it so, rather than because he himself finds it upsetting. Children begin to realize the differences in diagnoses at about the age of 7. Not all sicknesses are alike, they begin to understand. In the presence of a 3-year-old child, staff and family can discuss diagnosis, prognosis, therapy, and the impact of the child's impending death in front of him and he will remain impervious. An older child will grasp the import of the discussion and will be frightened by what he hears. The older child realizes the impact illness will have on his life, his independence, and his place in the world. He understands what he is losing.

It is frightening for the school-age child to come to the realization that his or her existence is threatened. She worries about how her existence will end, and time begins to have meaning. Because she regards the prognosis more as a certainty than a statement of possibility, the child is usually anxious to talk about and explore the meaning of death. She wonders if parents will share information with her. Does it mean they do not love her if they do not do so? Can she be replaced? Will she be quickly forgotten?

Seven- and eight-year-old children, and some even younger, are often very familiar with the disease process. At the very least they may know that leukemia is a blood problem, cancer isn't always curable, muscular dystrophy is crippling, and cystic fibrosis causes breathing problems. Many children have the knowledge and resourcefulness to search out information regarding the diagnosis. They may read all the literature they can obtain. Any attempts to hide facts may simply redouble their efforts to find answers. For instance, one 11-year-old boy concealed a tape recorder in his room because, he told a staff member, "people are more honest when you aren't around."

Some children accurately arrive at their diagnosis before they are admitted or referred. "I knew I had leukemia before I came. I studied it in science and I had all the symptoms."

Most children, however, experience the same shock and denial over the diagnosis as their parents. Frequently the older child goes from shock to anger and denial to embittered acceptance. "You're right, this life is not for me," he says belligerently. Emotional reactions to the diagnosis are often so mixed that it is difficult to distinguish anger from denial or guilt from depression. Initially the child may be convinced that the illness is punitive—the result of some past misdeed. He begins to search for a cause of the illness. When contagion is ruled out, the child may admit to the fear that the illness is a form of punishment. The concepts of self and illness often blur. The symbolic significance of the illness as much as its physical nature are serious concerns to some children. They may ask, "Does illness mean I'm bad?" "Did I do something wrong—is that why I'm sick?" An adult who is important to and trusted by the child should give reassurances that the illness does not stem from misbehavior. Typically such assurances produce a dramatic sigh of relief. "You mean I worried all these months for nothing?" said one youth who thought his testicular cancer was the result of masturbating.

Despite the older child's ability and desire to understand, it is often difficult for the parents to respond to the child's needs. Even close families who were accustomed to dealing with problems openly before the diagnosis find it difficult to continue to do so. In general, the stress of terminal illness does not bring families together — it divides them. With all the pressures the parents of a dying child have to endure, the prospect of facing the child's disappointments on a regular basis is often intolerable. Understandably, the distinction between which approaches are psychologically helpful to the patient and which are convenient deceits to protect the parents is not always clear. A breakdown in communication almost always occurs.

If an older child is discouraged from talking, asking for detailed factual information of his pathology, or sharing his fears and frustrations as well as his depression over his impending death, the child may die in emotional isolation. In an extreme case of parent protectiveness, Nan, a 15-year-old girl, became increasingly troubled by her mother's refusal to talk about her illness and impending death. The girl had not been told of the diagnosis until her third hospital admission. "I know I'm going to die," she told a staff member. "I want to talk to Mother, but she won't let me. I know she's hurting, but I'm the one who's dying." The staff approached the mother, trying to give support. The mother responded angrily, "She wouldn't be thinking of dying if you hadn't made her talk about it." Bitter episodes of fighting continued between the mother and her daughter until the daughter finally became severely depressed and withdrawn, whereupon her mother began speaking to her in baby talk. "Her doesn't feel goody today. Her doesn't want anybody around. Her hungry. Her doesn't want to talk." Although the girl did not return to school for an entire year, her mother did not inform the school of her illness, nor did she tell her own employer, relatives, or even the girl's older brother. To the end, the mother steadfastly refused to allow her daughter to disclose her feelings. When the girl died the mother felt satisfied that she had done what was best for her daughter and had given her proper support. She could not understand her daughter's need to talk about impending death.

When the family no longer provides answers to a child's questions, the child knows there is reason to be alarmed but doesn't know how to break the silence.

We've always done everything with each other knowing what was going on. Suddenly that was different. That scared me more than what was happening to my body. It felt like my family was becoming strangers. I had to set them straight. It was better after that.

Our family never talks. You never know what's going on. I knew it would be more of the same. I had to find out something so I waited and watched which person (staff) I thought I could talk to.

The older child needs her parents for support and security, but she also needs explanations of what is happening. Her independence is taken away in a variety of ways. In many cases, she finds out after everyone else that a procedure, a new protocol, new therapy, or delayed dismissal is being considered. "It's not fair," the child protests, "it's my body they're doing it to." Although the child will scold her parents, she may continue to smile at the staff making rounds. She is hurt, but she is also fearful of being totally excluded from decision-making processes in the future.

For some children, the ability to exercise control over anything happening to them seems to be lost when they are admitted to the hospital. At that time they give up their clothes, their privacy, the normal routines of their life. They are forced to accept meals when the hospital wants them to eat, they are told when to eliminate, and even though they are NPO (nothing by mouth) or are given enemas or laxatives, they may not be informed about procedures; they may even be blamed for failures (e.g., moving during a tap, or twitching and infiltrating an IV) or, on occasion, ridiculed for behavior considered inappropriate.

The course of an illness may be long and painful. At times it seems both endless and senseless to both parents and child. When the illness is an extended one, the procedures are generally more frequent, complicated, and prone to failure, and life becomes more dismal and depressing for parents and patients. The procedures designed to decrease or alleviate pain are often painful in themselves, e.g., multiple injections needed to start an IV for morphine, or draw blood for samples. Procedures such as spinal taps, bone marrow aspirations, venipunctures, or biopsies are rarely simple or painless for the patient.

I don't see the one who writes the orders and makes the generous remarks on rounds while they're trying. They keep saying, there's nothing to it—it's okay. It'll be over in a minute. It took 3 hours to start this IV. It took an hour and a half for the bone marrow and they finally had to do a biopsy. There's only one way it'll end. I don't have a way out.

Unfortunately, little can be done to change this course of events. Even if all procedures were discontinued, death would rarely occur soon afterwards.

Discipline and truthfulness are the only means of providing some normalcy and hope in the child's life. They also constitute the main ingredients of security. Giving a child special attention is not effective, since children want to be themselves.

I was embarrassed they treated me so good, I wanted things normal. I thought, the rest of the family is starting to hate you. They won't remember you for how nice you were but for all the favors you got. I hated that. I finally told Mom and she was shocked. She cried and said she didn't know what to do. She hated all that was happening. I told her I didn't want to be any different than the rest of the kids. I'm different enough with all this.

Older, school-age children know the behavior that is expected in return for being given honest answers and complete information. They know, for instance, how to express emotions and how to behave around various people so as to be judged competent and mature enough to deserve inclusion in discussions. The independence they strive for, however, is lost when the emotions or immaturity of others place them in dependent roles. If the demands of parents, staff, culture, religion, community, etc., are unacceptable to the child, he may find himself emotionally or even physically abandoned.

Unless the health care team specifically takes steps to erase the impression that the child's dignity is being stripped away, she or he may see this as happening. Emotionally and physically, the child is expected to endure the treatment and regimen imposed on her as if she were an adult. However, excluding her from playing a role in her own care, refusing to answer questions honestly, or manipulating her to elicit a certain response or behavior are all ways of treating her like a child. Condescending treatment is especially hard for boys to deal with. They may be driven to overcompensate by behavior detrimental to their condition, for example, playing rough sports, or refusing analgesics to prove their indifference to pain. A sick boy may even threaten suicide if more restrictions are placed upon him. One sensitive youth flew into a rage when an item on his bill listed something marked "baby needs." "They treat me like one, and write it down, too," he fumed.

The child's cooperation is compulsory for expedient therapy. Guilt about being ill in the first place, as well as about the effects the sickness is having on parents and family, is sometimes extreme. Frequently a child faces the cruel remarks of peers: "Hey, aren't you the one with cancer? My mom says you're gonna die." Or a girl may become a figure of fun because alopecia forces her to wear a wig, or amputation to use a prosthesis. The attention the school-age child needs now centers only on pain and illness. She lost her feeling of individuality and uniqueness during hospitalization because in the hospital she is a patient rather than a person.

The distasteful aspects of normal school and home life seem trivial compared with the isolation and restrictions imposed by illness.

I look at my friends and they don't have to face anything like this. They don't have anything like this. They complain about the dumbest things. I sure would trade with any of them any time.

The child tries to hide from the more painful aspects of attention – the annoying signals that she is different. It is particularly hard when adults stare.

They're worse than the kids. The kids ask outright. The adults stand there with their big mouths open. Sometimes I feel like making funny movements and sounds so they'd think I was having a fit.

All of which makes it difficult for the child to ignore her physical appearance.

"I look down and see all those bones and think, that's your skeleton. You already look like a corpse."

If the child's peers are unaware of her illness, their ridicule may be a repayment for what they consider the special treatment she receives. In other cases, the game of wig pulling seems genuinely funny. A child who vomits in public – a common secondary reaction to therapy – may also have an audience laughing at her misery. In an open setting, where fellow patients are coping with similar problems, it is easier for the child to put the illness and the response of outsiders to it in perspective. Because illness makes the child different, her contacts and friends change accordingly. Former friends may abandon her for fear of saying or doing the wrong thing, fear of contagion, or any number of real or imaginary fears. The sick child's new friends are usually fellow patients who have similar interests and problems. Together they can share their fears, frustrations, and painful experiences, and discuss their relationships with family, staff, and others, as well as their philosophies of life and death. Together they learn to cope.

As death approaches, children usually choose one or two persons with whom they want to share feelings. They do not want false cheerfulness or lugubrious scenes. Children appreciate an adult who is comfortable in an atmosphere of silence–a person who does not expect the child to talk. Because he is angry, hurting, or sick, a child may not feel like talking. If he feels comfortable enough with the adult in his presence to remain silent, that adult can regard this behavior as a compliment, for it is the height of acceptance. "When people feel uncomfortable, they really gab," one youth observed. Constant chatter can be a form of torture for a sick person.

It is often in the very terminal phase that the older child, knowing he will never get well, wishes his death would come. Some resist to the end, but this is rare. Because the child is usually resigned to his death before the family, role reversal often occurs, and the child shows amazing strength. One child whose parents could no longer tolerate the pain of the visits after many episodes of near-death told them to stay home with the younger children and attend to other family responsibilities. "I know I'm loved."

Older children worry about what the illness is doing to their families. They may fear that their illness is the cause of parents' marital problems, or of financial strain, even to the point of hiding symptoms to prevent procedures, an early admission, or a long-distance telephone call to the physician. They see siblings being neglected, parents skipping meals when visiting the hospital to save money, or sleeping in chairs in the waiting rooms because the cost of a motel room is too expensive. Often the child's guilt is openly expressed; "If it would do any good that would be fine. But it's like throwing money down the drain."

Many children thank their parents for all they have done for them, or ask forgiveness for transgressions or for the problems their illness has caused.

Chapter 3

Special Children

His affectionate behavior is considered typical of mongoloid children. With his heart defect and his clumsiness, he couldn't have kept up with the other children even if he tried let alone attack them. He never bothered their children and the children were very good to him. They seemed to realize that he had special problems. It was the parents who were hung up.

Two categories of special children are discussed in this chapter. The first is the child with a predisposing, non-life-threatening condition that demanded special attention and concern prior to the diagnosis of an incurable illness or to sudden death. The second is the child from a setting that makes him unique: the child of foreign descent, the adopted child, the only child, the twin.

The conditions that affect children in the first category (e.g., congenital anomalies, genetic defects, mental retardation, undergoing surgery, chronic bouts with infection) are not incompatible with life but they present major problems from the physical, emotional, financial, or mental standpoints. In some cases, living with a severe ongoing problem creates more physical and emotional distress than death itself.

One staff physician whose subspecialty was children with birth defects said to another staff member who cared for children with a high mortality rate, "Sometimes I think you are luckier. Your children die. Most of mine do not. I see the heartache that some of these families go through for years with no improvement in sight or possible. I don't mean it in a cruel, uncaring way. But some things are worse than death. It is death to a normal way of life for all of those involved."

PHYSICALLY HANDICAPPED CHILDREN

Any child born with a congenital anomaly is a worry to his parents. No matter how insignificant the anomaly is said to be, it does not seem so to the hypercritical eyes of new parents. When the dream of perfection is shattered, it sometimes yields to the obsession that more undiscovered defects may be present. An opposite reaction may also take place. Depending on the nature of the anomaly and the extent to which it is apparent, parents may refuse to accept the diagnosis. Cardiac anomalies, for instance, which cannot be seen and which produce no demonstrable differences in the child's appearance, are difficult for many parents to cope with. An anomaly that is not readily detectable to a nonmedical eye is also difficult to accept. If a parent cannot see the anomaly he or she may deny its seriousness or even its existence. Some parents find it more difficult to deal with an unknown than the "awful thing you can see." As one father said, "I would rather it be something I could see, then I would know what I was fighting and how bad it was. I have to rely on doctors now and they don't often agree among themselves."

Some parents vehemently deny that anything is wrong with their infant, or conceal or minimize the symptoms. The denial in such cases only heightens the problem and results in withdrawal by all concerned. If they withdraw, parents are forced to carry their grief alone. Even when they do not alienate themselves, it is not uncommon for the parents to find themselves abandoned almost immediately by friends and acquaintances. The word of their misfortune travels fast. After the preliminary condolences, other people may avoid them for fear of saying the wrong thing or even of placing themselves in the awkward position of having to pay the usual compliments about the infant. In other cases the parents' reticence makes it difficult for outsiders to approach them.

Constant sympathy can, however, be as great a problem as abandonment. Some parents complain that persistent lamentations and condolences makes rearing a child in a normal atmosphere impossible. Similarly, unabashed stares and unwanted attention makes anonymity impossible.

The looks people give us just makes me want to throw something at them. I just get furious. That is what my child has to face the rest of his life. It would have been easier if he died at birth than to have to face all this, except that he is so special and has such a personality that I don't think I could give him up.
                                                —Mother of a child with hydrocephalus.

The added guilt many parents feel when they wish the child would die is a heavy burden.

There were times when I didn't want him and then there were times when he was so lovable that I knew he was really special and I'd hate to have anything happen to him. I had mixed feelings about his diagnosis (cancer)—shock, guilt and relief. I thought, thank God, it wasn't any of our normal children. Now I feel horrible guilt because a human being deserves life.
—Mother of a retarded child.

Because of continual daily grief experienced by some parents, in addition to the overwhelming responsibilities of providing for the child, such thoughts are often unavoidable. Some parents burdened with the constant care of a child with severe physical handicaps cannot admit their feelings of embarrassment and shame except after extensive therapy. Their true feelings may be masked behind a show of equanimity:

I was given this cross to bear and I'll carry it. The word institution makes me quake. It's like I didn't care about my child and then abandoned her. I couldn't stand to do that. Anyway she is so cuddly, I love her more than any of my other children. She has been given to me for a special reason and I'll keep her at home. No doctor or social worker is going to convince me that I can't or shouldn't care for her. She has made me a better mother. I don't know what I did before she came to us.

The child who discovers he is different will find it difficult to cope with his misfortune without the help of parents. However, some parents do not allow the child to be normal, choosing instead to protect him and to deny the problem. Parents experience and relive the shock of their situation over and over again. Frequently the pressure of the outside world—the open-mouthed stares of people—prevents them from making the adjustment to a normal life.

The parents' attitudes make a tremendous difference in determining how the child adapts to his or her problem. Severely mentally retarded and emotionally disturbed children have more difficulty with adjustments. Children suffering physical disfigurement and defects badly need the family's support. Without it, they may suffer from emotional problems that are more damaging than the physical defect. A child with a cleft lip or a facial birthmark can be completely disabled by emotional problems if he is not permitted to develop a positive self-image.

With the help of family, friends, and staff, a child can adjust much better than an adult in the same situation. Although our culture puts a high value on physical beauty and mental acuity, we nevertheless recognize and appreciate special talents and unique qualities in an individual. Such talents give one a sense of self-esteem, and the strength and ability to cope.

The child who is denied proper support may be forced to manipulate the family in order to get the attention he craves. Often in such situations the parents' guilt makes discipline impossible. But just as a terminally ill child loses respect for himself and his parents when they suspend discipline, so, too, does the child with a handicap. He can become frightened, angry, and miserable, and feel that no one cares for or about him. He may be difficult for even his own family to tolerate, for reasons other than his handicap. Parents often verbalize their submission with remarks such as: "I know he's difficult, but there's nothing I can do. I feel sorry for him. I know I've created a brat but I feel too guilty to punish and discipline him." Some parents need professional help before they are able to express appropriate anger at their handicapped child.

When he had a temper tantrum he had a habit of biting the person he was angry at. I picked him up and said he wasn't allowed to do that anymore. I spanked him hard, harder than I thought I would. He and his brother looked totally dumbfounded. He cried and screamed. He later hugged me. I felt guilty, pleased, and good all at the same time. I've done it two more times since. He's a different boy now and I'm a different mother.

Hereditary problems frequently cause parents to feel guilty. If permitted to do so, the child can use the guilt as a means of getting back at parents if he does not get his way.

You caused this to happen to me. Now you better suffer with me. Why do I have to be the one?

In such cases, parents need not only genetic counseling but the intervention of professionals to help them adjust to a normal life. The parents need to reassure the child by expressing their sadness but also their confidence that the child can adjust with their support, and that his life can be a reasonably normal one.

MENTALLY RETARDED CHILDREN

The care of mentally retarded children presents many problems which, depending upon the extent of their handicap, may be more difficult to deal with than physical problems. For one thing, there is often more support available to families of children with physical problems than those with mental ones. In addition, their communicative skills may be extremely limited, and their activity range may vary from nearly fetal positioning to hyperactivity. Usually these children are rejected and feared to a greater extent than those who suffer physical disabilities.

Parents of mentally retarded children are hurt by the indifference they encounter. They do not feel others appreciate the love they have for their child nor the love they get in return. Nor do people appreciate the complications of caring for such children, or the milestones the children reach regardless of how far behind other children they are developmentally.

Parents encounter callous individuals who suggest that caring for a mentally retarded child who has been diagnosed with a fatal illness is a waste. They rarely hear anyone bluntly suggest that they "get rid of the problem," yet many parents believe that other people think this way. To an unperceptive outsider the diagnosis of a fatal illness or the death of this type of child is often seen as a relief. The families of mentally retarded children report that few outsiders express sympathy for the loss of the child.

Typically, such families find limited emotional support. Parents need to verbalize their feelings of disgust at the monumental tasks they face when their child has a fatal illness. They feel they must make up to the child what he has already been cheated of. Moreover, his handicap has taken their time and energies away from their normal healthy children and removed from their lives the semblance of normalcy that other parents take for granted. They are angry at the unfairness of so much misfortune being directed at one unfortunate child.

Some parents express relief that the child cannot understand what is taking place. They do not have to face the questions about the diagnosis and impending death as parents of normal children do. At the same time, they feel frustrated that they have to give total support, since the child receives none from his peers.

Mental retardation that occurs as a result of an accident, infection, or disease usually compounds the grief of parents when the child is dying. In effect, they lose the child twice. They experience all the shock and anger of parents whose child has been retarded since birth, but in a much briefer span of time, and then death itself.

EMOTIONALLY HANDICAPPED CHILDREN

The emotionally handicapped child has unique problems that manifest themselves in many activities and behaviors. The hyperactivity, fetal positioning, or inappropriate behavior (hitting, biting, kicking, swearing, screaming, exhibitionism, masturbation, peculiar speech patterns, self-mutilation, etc.) are embarrassing and frustrating to the parents. Frequently these children are difficult to deal with, and, because of their problems, they may be inaccessible. Some emotionally handicapped children also appear retarded because of their problems. They may be handled at home or have day care, hospital care, or institutionalization. The latter alternatives may be the source of both relief and guilt. Medication and behavioral modification techniques are often useful provided they are prescribed by a professional whose instructions are followed by the family.

In some cases, the family may be the causal factor of the child's illness. One severely emotionally disturbed child was institutionalized, much to the relief of the parents. When the child later died from self-inflicted injuries, the parents felt his "disease and craziness"resulted from God's punishment. This child was conceived out of wedlock, and the parents felt that their sin would be absolved through their suffering his "craziness" and death. The child provided the desired punishment and absolution.

ADOPTED CHILDREN

Adopted children are often called "special children" in the sense that they were chosen. Parents usually feel a particular responsibility toward them because their inclusion in the family was deliberate. It is common for adoptive parents to feel that they asked for specific problems of parenthood, in contrast to natural parents, whom they feel had the option of whether or not to conceive. In many cases, adoptive parents feel they have no right to complain.

Because they asked for the responsibility of parenthood, the adoptive parents often feel they should be "superparents." At the time of diagnosis of terminal illness, many adoptive parents express the feeling that the situation is unfair to both natural and adoptive parents. "We love her so. Her natural parents will never know." They may express frustration because they do not know the child's full medical history, and in some instances, guilt that they did not probe more thoroughly. In their anger they often blame the natural parents, but such anger is commonly followed by guilt; they are aware that, had it not been for the natural parents, they would have remained childless.

The adopted child also feels the responsibility for being different and may want to protect his parents. Such reactions are especially common during adolescence. The child may blame the natural parents or, in a state of anger, may blame the adoptive parents for not being able to prevent the diagnosis by early detection. She or he usually feels guilt immediately or soon after, however, begins to realize the burden the illness imposes on the parents, and feels a particular responsibility to make life easier for them. Such protectiveness is more common in an adopted than in a natural child, and may also extend to the natural parents if the child feels they might suffer too much if they knew he was ill. Rarely do adopted children escape concern over the identity of their real parents. Typically they spend time speculating on the impact their illness would have on their real parents if they knew. "Would they visit if they knew of my terminal illness?" "What would they look like?" "How would they behave?"

The adoptive parents may share some of these concerns. They may wrestle with the problem of whether to notify (or attempt to notify) the real parents. Sometimes they think the child himself will want to meet the real parents, but they reject the idea immediately on the grounds that they may lose the child to his real parents. To some adoptive parents the thought of facing the natural parents is an unpleasant one because they feel it would underscore their own failure, that is, their inability to have children in the first place. Perhaps motivated by the unconscious fear that someone will prove them unfit for continuing to care for the child, the adoptive parents often emphasize their intense love for their child. In some cases these fears are verbalized, usually producing a salutary effect.

Adoptive parents are no different from natural parents with regard to the ambivalence they feel toward the terminally ill child. However, few are able to discuss their feelings. In most cases the adoptive parents are so absorbed in trying to fulfill the role of superparents that they dare not admit their ambivalence. They complain less at first, but when finally expressed, their feelings are the same as those of natural parents. They are confronted with others telling them how lucky the child is to have them and how much love they must feel if they voluntarily became parents. In fact, some adoptive parents contribute to this sentiment by making statements like, "I wish I didn't love so much," as if to imply that the capacity of an adoptive parent to love is somehow different from that of a natural one.

CHILDREN FROM ONE-PARENT FAMILIES

Children who have lived through the divorce of their parents have already experienced some grief. When parents were uncomfortable living together before the separation, and the tension was apparent to the children, the separation or divorce is in some ways a relief; nevertheless, it creates mixed feelings in the minds of the children. In cases where little discord was apparent before, the child finds it more difficult to accept the loss of a parent, particularly if he was close to that parent. When one parent leaves, quickly remarries, and begins living a new family life, the child feels even more rejected.

Typically the children of divorced parents feel unworthy of love, and to such children the diagnosis of a fatal illness may be the proof, the punishment they feel they deserve. As one teen-ager expressed it, "This is one more proof that I'm lousy." Moreover, most children fear that somehow they may have caused their parents to separate.

Children of one-parent families created by death often feel they should be the emotional support for the surviving parent. Throughout the course of their terminal illness they see the remaining parent reexperiencing the feelings of grief that he or she has already suffered.

He (a 9-year-old boy) keeps trying to be the father of the family and always so brave. That makes me feel so bad. He knows I cry easily. He keeps telling me I shouldn't. Daddy will take care of us from heaven and he'll do it down here. Then I really cry. I feel like we all have to play such a protection game.

It is not uncommon for children to assume a role equivalent to that of "superparent" in trying to give support to a single parent. One adolescent boy whose mother died after he was diagnosed matured rapidly. He wanted frequent passes from the hospital to be with his father, and when home he worked hard around the house. He no longer complained about procedures, school problems, or the other responsibilities that he had found so restrictive prior to his mother's death.

CHILDREN OF FOREIGN DESCENT

America prides itself on being a melting pot. Nevertheless our society comprises a variety of subcultures, of ethnic groups with customs, values, and traditions that are unfamiliar to many people outside the particular subculture. An innocent mistake by a nurse or a member of the health care team can jeopardize the care of a patient who comes from a different background. Many of the traditions, beliefs, and rituals of a particular group are potentially significant for the patient's well-being, and need the understanding of the staff.

One gypsy family refused surgery on one of their tribe because such a procedure undertaken at any other time except the night of a full moon was considered unlucky. The doctor waited until the full moon before performing the necessary surgery. Another family, believing in the medicinal power of spices and herbs and the restorative power of certain rituals, received the cooperation of the staff, who allowed some aspects of the patient's culture to be incorporated into his professional care. Such compromises should not be made insincerely or in a condescending manner. Rather, they should be arrived at on the basis of the following considerations: the patient's and the family's peace of mind, the staff's intent to show good faith, and the patient's well-being.

When parents and child enter the strange environment of a hospital, they have to contend with intimidating equipment, painful and restricting procedures, and rules, regulations, and explanations that they do not always understand. They need support, understanding, and explanations of what is going on in order to feel comfortable. The staff should make these overtures to gain the confidence of the parents and child.

One Mexican-American family, who spoke very little English, was not around when their infant's condition worsened. They had no telephone and could not be reached. On an earlier occasion, the resident had explained intravenous therapy to the parents, at which time they gave consent for it. Thus, when the IV in the infant's arm infiltrated, a scalp vein was used, and a patch of the infant's hair was shaved to insert the IV. When the parents arrived the following day they saw the shaved portion and immediately became upset. In their culture, cutting an infant's hair before his first birthday was thought to cause blindness. Because of the family's anxiety, coupled with the language barrier (despite the earnest efforts of a Spanish-speaking resident) no communication was possible. The parents were convinced that the child would be blind. The staff felt that after the initial misunderstanding the family lost all faith in them. The family refused to discuss their child's condition even with a Spanish-speaking doctor.

Even with the support of the health care team, situations such as the above do arise for which the staff is unprepared. Because of ignorance of the particular subculture or language, it may be extremely difficult for staff to deal with the family without the intervention of someone who can mediate.

Likewise, the child who has grown up with the demands of a particular culture has adjusted to them and accepts them obediently. Although these demands may not seem appropriate to an outsider—that is, one from a different culture—it is essential that they be understood. A part of any child's maturation is his awareness of social roles and his adoption of the values of his culture.

TWINS

The attention that surrounds the parents of twins makes this one of the most interesting, yet frustrating, experiences of parenting; it is all the more so with identical twins. The comparisons normally made between siblings of a family, their appearance, intelligence, personalities, talents, or the way they dress, acquire a special mystique when the siblings are twins. Twins draw attention because they *are* twins, and a part of that attention takes the form of encouragement to be alike. Even when their sameness is not encouraged, their two lives become one. It is natural to have one's likeness around, unnatural when he is not around.

When one of the pair becomes seriously ill or is severely injured, many of the similarities are replaced by frightening contrasts. The sick twin and the well one are now regarded differently.

It is especially difficult for twin children under the age of 4 to understand the concept of permanent separation, particularly when the death of a twin occurs as a result of accident or the quick onset of an illness. Sensitive questions about the sick sibling are often evaded as if his identity had disappeared beyond recall.

Both the twin diagnosed with a terminal illness and the well twin find that people look at them differently, sometimes fearfully. The healthy twin begins to fear the same thing that happened to his twin will happen to him. He may even fear he caused the accident or illness.

Parents of identical twins legitimately fear for the well twin following the diagnosis of a terminal illness. In some instances, the parents' fears are increased after learning the diagnosis because they have been told, or thought they had been told, that their twins were identical. Like any parent, they fear the disease could be repeated in the family, but the fear is greater in a family with twins. Statistics mean little in overcoming many fears. Even the well twin may ask, "If he dies does that mean I do, too?" Medical tests conducted to rule out the presence of disease or defect often only serve to confirm to him that parents and doctors do consider him in danger!

The well twin may suffer profound loneliness during the separation caused by hospitalization. As the illness progresses and the sick twin becomes more and more changed in appearance and behavior, the well child's sense of loss is severe. If he knows, or thinks he knows, that his twin will die, his grief in anticipation of losing his lifelong companion and "other half" is extremely painful and probably unique.

> People keep comparing him still (after the death of the twin). I can tell after they do that he flounders and becomes depressed and agitated. He has picked up a lot of what his brother liked to do, but he has become more independent. He was the follower. He was lost during Brad's illness and was shoved to the background. He had a hard time learning to play with other children because they were so close and liked the same kind of things. Neither had many outside friends.

The sick twin also has a difficult time. The frequent comparisons of the past disappear and he becomes more of an individual in his own right, but in ways that are unpleasant. He receives an abundance of attention because his illness demands it. He is angry at the fact that he is the twin who faces hospitalizations, clinic visits, pain, and the indignities of illness. It isn't fair, he says, when he is alone in suffering such things as hair loss, weight loss or gain, therapeutic side effects, or the debilitation of the disease process. More than other dying children he sees what he is leaving behind, comparing his decline with his twin's continuing normal life.

THE ONLY CHILD

The only child is special because he has no competition. Whether his unique status was the deliberate choice of his parents or resulted from their inability to have other children matters little. Since he does not have to compete with siblings for love and attention, the only child is the center of the family circle.

The diagnosis of terminal illness or the sudden death of the child is apt to be more painful for the parents of an only child. Whether the parents are unable to have more children, or have elected to have just one child, the effect is the same; they now see themselves as permanently childless.

> I know I couldn't go through an abortion, and yet, I couldn't go through another child having this illness. I guess I'm really in a bind. I am healthy and could have children. We both love them so much. However, I'm not taking any chances of going through this again. I don't think I'm stable enough. So here I am, childless after our loss.

Very often after the death of an only child a parent will say, "He was my whole life."

> If there was ever a child wanted and loved, it was our Dicky. We worked hard and hoped that he wasn't a spoiled brat. Many people told us he was one of the nicest boys they had ever met and that was before he was diagnosed. It's especially hard when your whole reason for living is not living anymore.

Some only children are the result of the parents' effort to bring an unhappy marriage together. In such cases the child is often used as a pawn. Typically, the unhappy parents try to outdo each other in the competition to become the child's "best pal" or favorite parent. In one instance, a couple with serious marital problems made the child a participant in their disputes. Each day the child received a bigger and better gift from each parent. Since the child was indifferent to the gifts, the parents sought arbitrators. They would show the staff what each of them had given the child. "These are *my* toys," the father proudly told a staff member one day.

Children who have been sheltered may have a more difficult time being separated from parents, adjusting to hospitalization, sharing toys and attention, or having other children around when they were accustomed to privacy. The adult attention the child previously received now comes from many different persons, most of them strangers. In a world so different from the one in which he exercised a fair amount of control, the only child may need more understanding and help than a child who has brothers and sisters at home.

Part Two

The Grievers

Chapter 4

Parents

You have no idea of the tension a family lives with when a child is going to die. You feel guilty at every turn. If you don't, others make sure you do.

I keep trying to make something good out of all this pain. I keep telling myself how nice everybody has been and the friends I've met through the experience. I think of how great that boy of mine was when a lot of parents have nothing but problems with theirs. That doesn't give me back my boy. It makes me want him all the more. I think, at least I had him. Then I feel guilty.

So I go to hell for not believing. I have news for you. I'm already there.

Following the diagnosis of fatal illness, stresses begin to exert themselves on the parents. It would be difficult to imagine a more painful role than that of parent to a dying child. Feeling hopelessly guilty, bombarded with advice, hemmed in by restrictions, demands, and obligations from which there is no avenue of escape, the parent must somehow or other keep functioning.

Regardless of how stable the marital relationship was before the diagnosis, it will be tested to the limit in the course of the illness and the postdeath period.

We haven't had any major things go wrong with Hank since he was diagnosed. I dread to think what is ahead. We seem to have no affection for each other. It's as if we were strangers. The only thing we talk about is Hank's illness and progress. We haven't slept together for so long I can't remember. It's scary and lonely. All the kids are getting on our nerves. I'm afraid and angry. I'm beginning to resent my husband *and* Hank. I wish it was all over with, but after it is, I won't have anything. At least now I have Hank. He appreciates and loves me. The other kids do well when I'm not at home.

I thought the diagnosis would bring us together. It seemed to at first. I guess it was guilt over not wanting the pregnancy. It didn't take long for the hassles to begin all over again. I don't know which would be worse, staying and fighting, feeling angry all the time, or separating and feeling guilty.

Throughout the course of the illness, the parents face continual changes: of identity, goals, standard of living, plans. It is virtually impossible for them to prepare for a future they do not really believe exists. Family members may live together like strangers, unsure how to relate.

Anger and confusion may be constant states of mind. To the parents their behavior and their feelings seem abnormal. When they read newspaper stories about other couples who are presumably doing well, while living through a similar experience, the parents feel more depressed, inadequate, and guilty. "Am I normal?" "Am I crazy?" are questions they continually ask.

Parents feel they must manage their emotions at all times and maintain an image of strength. Ironically, a great number of parents have a fear of breaking down, yet feel anger because their spouse shows so little emotion. This example typifies the misunderstandings that result from a breakdown in communication between the parents. Communication is difficult because most feelings during periods of great stress tend to be negative: guilt, blame, depression, denial. Discussion at a feeling level is sharply curtailed so that with every new stage of illness the understanding of each other's feelings diminishes. At a certain point in the child's illness, many families cease to communicate altogether. Instead they resort to intuition which, invariably, is faulty.

I thought my wife didn't care about me. She didn't seem to care about the other kids. I felt totally useless as a husband and father. I felt depressed but little emotion. My wife said I was selfish. I started to believe it. I wanted her attention, but then I'd feel awful because the only way I'd get it would be Rudi's death. We never talked until a long time after the funeral. I wish we had talked during his illness. We would have both realized we felt almost the same.

PARENTS' ROLES

The socioeconomic status of the family will be the basis for many of the decisions made in the course of the child's illness. The family whose resources are limited may be forced to have therapy performed by someone in their community because commuting long distances, eating out, or spending days or weeks in motels or boarding houses are all too expensive. The amount of time the parents can spend with the child may also depend on their finances.

Preestablished notions of what is expected of each and of what they should derive from the relationship usually do not change as a result of the diagnosis and illness. The parent who is the organizer or the decision maker usually behaves in character throughout the illness. The same consistency applies to negative coping mechanisms, which, even if they do not offer solace, are nonetheless firmly entrenched. For example, if one's coping mechanism is to drink, this will not change; in fact, the drinking will probably increase.

The support needed by each parent varies according to the particular situation. What is supportive to one parent may not be to another. In some instances one parent may require a generous amount of support from hospital staff, while the other prefers to be left alone. An outsider intent on giving support should be aware of when it is appropriate, and when unwelcome.

MOTHERS

Enlightened attitudes toward the role of women both in and out of the home usually vanish when the woman is the mother of a terminally ill child. She is expected to become the primary source of care when the child suffers grave injuries or terminal illness. Occasionally the social pressures to become more involved are at odds with her own feelings. Her attitudes toward the support she should give her child and the type of care required may differ from the norm prescribed by tradition. Ultimately how comfortable she feels has much to do with how supportive the staff is.

It seems that, whatever the woman's philosophy, she is expected to become a "supermother" after the diagnosis. The outside pressure to continue doing everything she has been doing up until then, as well as to care for her child, is strong. An overwhelming sense of responsibility for the support and care of the child is thrust upon her whether she wants it or not, and whether or not she even enjoys the role of being a parent. To be other than a supermother is to be insensitive and neglectful.

Working and professional mothers often are forced to take a leave of absence, if not to leave their jobs completely. Periodic leaves may be compulsory for them throughout the course of illness. The child's condition, diagnosis, and prognosis, as well as economic factors, often dictate the decisions a mother makes.

Some women who produce an "imperfect" child feel sole responsibility. Guilt usually fuels the supermother syndrome, but all the efforts of a supermother cannot allay the guilt. She feels guilt no matter how she spends her time; for example, if she is with the sick child, she worries about the siblings "abandoned" at home.

No matter what you do, you feel like it's wrong. Nothing is comfortable. You're always in the wrong place. Your mind and body are never in the same place. You don't feel like you do a thing well. Your job suffers, all your kids suffer, your mate is abandoned, your family and friends wonder if you know who they are except in emergencies. You don't know what you're thinking except fear and confusion. You're exhausted and scared. You feel crazy, you're resentful being dependent, you feel selfish. Few people realize how appreciative you are because you're so short-tempered. You wish you weren't married or a parent. You feel guilty over everything you do or don't do. There's no end to this mess.

Many women, for the first time in their lives, begin to doubt their suitability for motherhood or even question their decision to become a mother in the first place. This is just another variation of the ambivalence parents feel during the illness: "Is it worth all this?" they ask.

Mothers who are rooming-in find themselves trying to maintain a reasonably normal household some distance away, and to meet all their regular responsibilities as well as take care of the child. The combination of being separated from the family, the transient lifestyle of rooming-in, and the feeling of being utterly at the mercy of conditions she has no control over accentuate the mother's misery.

Look at me. I haven't slept in four nights, taken a bath in two days, my hair hasn't been shampooed for a week. I'm a nervous wreck and I'm failing as a parent. No wonder my husband is ready to disown me, my kids don't care, and the sick child is so irritable.

I don't even feel like a woman. I'm losing part of my motherhood there in my child's bed. My husband probably can't remember when we were a couple and the other kids don't know their own mother. You not only lose a child when one is terminally ill, you lose your entire life.

FATHERS

The father of a terminally ill child is seldom required to play the correlative role of "superfather." Rather he is expected to be stoic, strong, and a good provider. The role is ultratraditional and rather cumbersome, but this is how the father often sees himself:

That's what men in our society stand for: fatherhood, provider, disciplinarian. I've failed at all of them. I can't even give emotional support to my wife and kids. The other day I cried.

The consequence of not being involved in the day-to-day care of an ill child is that the father often becomes physically and emotionally alienated from the family. When the child receives treatment away from home, the father may go for long periods of time without wife, child, relatives, or friends. Because of the distance he may have to travel, as well as economic considerations, demands at home, or even the emotional tension his presence creates when he does visit the hospital, visiting may be extremely difficult.

The father who has not cared for his child on a regular basis feels unskilled and inadequate, and defers to anyone who seems more competent than he. Simple ministrations may seem embarrassing or clumsy—soothing the child in the presence of strangers, or trying to perform aspects of the child's care that disrupt the routine. His ineptitude may incur the anger and resentment of the staff, his wife, or the child. Sometimes his visits interrupt the calmness of the routine or complicate the treatment and care. He is either cued or, in some cases, bluntly told to limit his visits. This makes one less person to deal with. The mother is then able to focus her attention on the sick child, and the staff can continue its work with the mother and child to whom they have become accustomed. Frequently the father needs support as well as permission to help in the care of his sick child. This may have to be initiated by the staff.

In some cases the father's experience with clinic visits, lab data, therapy results, side effects, or disciplinary problems does not start until the child goes home. His ignorance in all these matters seems to underscore his inadequacies as a parent: suddenly he is experiencing what his wife and child went through months before.

Because of financial hardship, many fathers take other jobs to cover escalating expenses. Undoubtedly a father would be made to feel guilty if he could not provide financial support, but even when he can, he often feels inadequate. Typical comments are: "It'd help if I felt I could do something other than pay the bills," or "The only time anybody seems to care if I'm around is when the goddamn business office wants me or the bills come."

STEPPARENTS

Stepparents are often reluctant to take on the role of a natural parent following the diagnosis for fear of causing hard feelings or falling into some of the negative stereotypes of stepparents. Sometimes the stepparent is thrust into the role of providing the primary care for the child because it has been abdicated by the natural parent. Having been pushed into the position, the stepparent may be resentful.

It is also possible that stepparents, like adoptive parents, feel none of these pressures. Even though the child is theirs only in a legal sense, they may make no distinction between the love they have for this child and for one of their own.

In cases where a stepparent and natural parent do not get along, yet are frequently around each other, an impossible situation may arise. The staff may have to intervene and, for the child's sake, impose what amounts to a code of conduct.

HAVING ANOTHER CHILD

Many parents want a child soon after the death, but they may be afraid to assume the responsibility. They are concerned about health problems occurring in any future children. Despite their desire to have another child right away, many parents report that they waited at least one year before starting the pregnancy, and that they are grateful they waited.

> I don't want to replace and of course I can't, but also I couldn't stand the emptiness. I realize that would have been a horrible mistake, but my arms ached to hold, to cuddle, to fondle a baby and be needed. My other children had grown up without me during the illness. I didn't feel needed. I thought an infant would fill that need. I would have made him a sick neurotic child, so, thank God, I didn't get pregnant when I wanted so badly to have someone to depend on me.

Parents may feel that they would like another child if they could choose the sex. They fear a child of the same sex would be thought of as a replacement, or that the child would be subject to constant comparison. Many children born subsequently are named after the dead sibling: Jamie for James, Melinda for Linda, Marybelle for Bill, Wilma for William. Parents sometimes use the child's middle name as the sibling's first name, or some variation of it to keep the name alive.

In some cases the role of the sibling is well defined. She will continue in the footsteps of the child who died. Many parents express the belief that the child born after diagnosis or death is a special child, "sent from God," "a lifesaver," a "reason for living," or a "savior of our marriage."

Special though the child may be, parents are often obsessed with dates and fearful that the anniversary of death and a birthday may be the same. Or they may fear that the future child will be born on the same date as their other child's funeral day, the day of relapse, or of the accident, and therefore be a continual painful reminder of what they received in exchange for what they lost.

They may be afraid that the unborn child will have the same physical features as the dead child or that its personality will constantly remind them of the one they loved and lost. Some fear that there will be no resemblance.

The thought of future pregnancies is frightening. Parents fear that subsequent children may be vulnerable to the same fatal illness or accident. But after the new child lives past the age of the one who died, they draw a sigh of relief: "Now he's 9 months old, 3 months older than John when he died." "He's 6 years old and hasn't been diagnosed with leukemia. I think we can breathe easier now."

Chapter 5

Siblings

I wish they'd be honest in how bad they hurt and how afraid they are. Then we could talk. I don't dare because they think they're making me feel better. We're just miserable. You ache to see your parents hurting so, and you can't do anything to help. You'd hate to destroy all that love they have. They think they're doing the best thing. They are for them. Nobody can be honest and open in this stupid society. It isn't fair — all this and then having to act on top of it.

If you're the sick one, everybody cares. If you're the brother or sister, they don't give a hoot.

I still have to go on living. We have other children who need us. When I see the kids play, I think of how much attention I gave Kurt, and I realize how much they have been cheated. I think I could understand their hating him. It wasn't their fault that he got sick.

As the sick child becomes the central figure in the family, all other members must take second place. Siblings are pushed to the background while parents devote their attentions to the sick child or to other concerns which, because of the illness, seem to take precedence over the well children.

The preeminent importance of the sick child's needs often means that the well children are forgotten. Their achievements are ignored, their recitals or sports contests are often not attended by parents. At times siblings may be forced to find proxy parents to attend a sports event or performance. They worry, they have fears, they feel guilty, and when they have no power to change the course of events, they become depressed.

The sick sibling at least has the attention of his parents and others, but the well child faces radical changes in his life without support. Anxiety is common when the family is physically separated by hospitalizations and clinic visits, but even when the family is together it is seldom emotionally united.

In families with no firsthand experience with death prior to the diagnosis of fatal illness, it is common for family members to experience an initial closeness. Gradually this yields to physical and emotional separation as the stresses increase. Only the family that is used to sharing its feelings and discussing its problems honestly is equipped to sustain closeness throughout the child's illness. Intellectualizing problems is sometimes mistaken for openness, but the difference between the two is the difference between sharing facts and sharing feelings. Sharing feelings is totally unacceptable to some parents. They may tolerate candor and spontaneity in young children but find them unacceptable from older ones.

Siblings are often protected from the truth of the sick child's prognosis because the parents do not think they can cope with the knowledge. The language they choose to explain the disruptions caused by illness may be devoid of any serious-sounding complications, but the parents' concern will still be transmitted to the other children. The parents' best intentions are almost certain to backfire: the well siblings suffer cruelly, but do not know why.

It is difficult for siblings of any age who are not fully informed of the illness to understand deviations from the normal routine. Why, for instance, is the sick sibling cuddled when he throws a temper tantrum? Why do the parents react with such vehemence when the well child takes a swat at his brother? The well child's generosity is tested to the limit when he is forced to cater to the sick child's wishes, humor him through bad moods and temper tantrums, allow him to play with whatever toys he commands, and suffer all his abuse with forbearance.

The relationship between siblings changes continuously throughout the course of an illness. What was a stormy relationship at the time of diagnosis may become a close one at the time of death. Whether from guilt, pressure from others to get along, or because of the time spent with the sibling during hospitalization, the relationship in some cases becomes a mutually supportive one.

I kept getting madder and madder at my brother. I couldn't stand all the attention he always got. Everybody made a fuss over him. He acted like an idiot some of the time. I also felt awful for getting so mad. One day I'd had enough. I really let him have it. Mom and Dad were gone or they would have croaked. I guess that was why I had the guts to really let loose. Man, I said things that I didn't know I'd ever say out loud. I ended up crying and telling him how bad I felt. We really talked. Since then he tells me I'm the only one he can talk to. I'm really glad it happened.

In other cases, however, a well child who fears the unknown about death —where, when, and how it will happen—wishes it were over so normalcy might return. Sharing these feelings with the family, however, may cause a tremendous outburst, and this, in turn, instills more guilt in the child.

SIBLINGS FEEL ANGER AND GUILT

Anger and guilt are common feelings in siblings who must watch someone else occupy the center of attention. Few people remember the well children when there is a terminally ill child in the family. Everyone is, understandably, concerned about how the sick child is doing, how his medicine is working, or when he is to go back to the hospital. Prior to the diagnosis, one of the "well" children in the family may have been suffering from asthma, allergies, or injuries which made him or her the center of attention. After the diagnosis, these problems may be partially or totally ignored by the parents. This angers the child, whose pain is real. Parents panic at the least complaint of the terminally ill child, even though it is sometimes obvious to the other children that the sick sibling is using his disease to get attention. The well children may even use the same complaints as the sick sibling, only to be rebuked for doing so.

The confusion of some children about what the illness means and how serious it is may be shown by their imitating the mannerisms of the sick child. If the sick child's appetite increases as a result of medication, the well child's appetite may also increase. The well child may limp, or else complain of headaches just as the sibling does after lumbar punctures. Or she may insist on taking vitamin pills to copy the sibling's ingestion of drugs.

When a healthy sibling has minor aches and pains, or the flu, or even a fracture, he or she is generally expected to bear this with very little sympathy. He may even be castigated for adding to the parents' troubles:

How could you be so clumsy and stupid? You should have known you'd get hurt. You know this is the first time we've had away from a hospital in weeks? Now we have to wait in the emergency room for you.

There are times when the well child may think he is more sick than the terminally ill child, if the latter is in remission. To him, there is little difference between his illness and his sibling's illness at that point, except that his sibling gets all the attention.

Because the well child's state of mind is taken for granted and so much is demanded of him, he may not have the opportunity to express anger or rid himself of guilt. Finally his feelings may break out in a devastating catharsis:

> I wish that brat would drop dead, then we would have a halfway normal home again. You never listen to anybody anymore, only his whining and complaining. There are other people in this house, but you wouldn't care if I dropped dead today as long as you could have that brat.

The well sibling who hears someone caution him that "someday you'll be sorry you said that," knows it is true. Someday he will relive the guilt and shame—probably many times over.

Anger and guilt may be inseparable during the course of the sibling's illness, but after the death, guilt begins to predominate: guilt for being healthy, guilt for being the survivor when he may feel he is the more expendable of the two. Moreover, the child who once wished he were an only child feels that by some magical process he has made the wish come true. Even adolescents may still believe in the magical powers of threats and selfish wishes.

The well child may feel guilty for having fun or making plans for the future. Even though she knows that she is not responsible for her sibling's illness, the resumption of a normal routine may seem wrong. Parents may reinforce this notion. "That's good. Such a pity your poor brother will never get to do that. You have so much. He has nothing and is losing everything." If she succeeds and achieves, she is living the chance denied the sick child. If she fails, she is not using her potential—one that was denied to the sick sibling. Adolescents rarely share with parents their disappointments, frustrations, and failures. They may turn for support instead to teachers, counselors, school nurses, other relatives, or hospital staff. They need someone who will listen without comment or judgment, or, if need be, offer objective comments about the child's predicament.

> I thought I was crazy. The only feelings I could feel for Dick were anger, jealousy, and hate. I felt guilt. It just kept getting worse. My teacher said I could talk any time. He wouldn't tell anybody. He understood because he had a sister die when he was a kid. He had the same feelings.

APPROACHES THAT CAN HELP

Siblings can be made to feel important, and their problems can be alleviated, if they are able to participate in the affairs of the family at the time of crisis. They should be allowed to help parents, their efforts to care for the sick child should be praised, and the hardships they endure acknowledged. If they are so encouraged, these children may help the family maintain a fairly normal way of life. In many families, the siblings take over routine chores such as housecleaning, meal preparation, or babysitting for young children or for the sick child. Children who never before displayed the inclination to pick up their clothes or cook a meal sometimes become great organizers in time of need. Before the crisis such jobs were odious, but now they represent a contribution to the household, something from which the child derives immense satisfaction.

Other useful ways to help siblings include allowing them to come to the clinic, or doctor's office, or to participate in groups that include other siblings. They can also be asked to join in small family decisions, such as the choice of a restaurant, decisions which are often left only to the sick child. Siblings can be introduced to hospital staff and become acquainted with the hospital environment, allowed to witness procedures and examinations, when deemed advisable, or to take tours of the hospital or clinic. After such experiences, they are quick to recognize what is at stake.

> I had no idea what it was like. I thought they had to see the doctor and then went shopping. I thought the stay in the motel would be fun. We couldn't play and the room was crowded. Jack became depressed and grumpy the night before he went to the doctor. I can understand now after seeing what he had to go through. It was awful. I'm glad I'm me. I could see my parents were upset, but they didn't say anything.

The fortunate sibling is the one who is included when the family goes to the hospital to visit the sick child, who helps pack before admissions and dismissals, and even goes with his or her parents to the business office; such a child is a colleague of the parents and a willing participant in the responsibilities of the family.

PEERS OF SIBLINGS

Siblings are placed in a difficult position at home; but even outside the home the stigma of disease may follow them. Peers can be supportive, but more often they bring added pressure, which increases the healthy sibling's anger, fear, and guilt.

The healthy sibling may be forced to defend his brother or sister when disease or disfigurement make the sick child the object of ridicule. He suffers embarrassment when his sibling misbehaves in public or in the presence of his friends. He is often ashamed of what has happened to his family. A friend may say:

> Your parents always had us over. They were at all the games and took us for hamburgers afterwards. How come they don't come anymore? Don't they care anymore?

> Boy, your Mom and Dad are grouchy. What did I do to make them so mad?

Rarely will the sibling turn to his parents with these complaints. He fears that he will simply add to their grief, and so carries the burden quietly and secretly.

Siblings face taunts from other children. Often these taunts persist until the sibling is able to stand up and face his accusers openly. Or, like the sick sibling, the well one may seek a new circle of friends who are more understanding and more tolerant of the pressures he is experiencing.

REACTIONS AFTER DEATH

The young child's first reaction to the death of a sibling may be, "Now I'm the oldest (youngest, middle)," or, "Now we have a family again," or "We can go out again," or "Don't feel bad, you have us." The most important things to him are the return to a normal life and getting back the attention and love he has missed.

Parents frequently compare the child's display of emotions (or more commonly the lack of any emotion) with their own reactions. This is not a fair comparison. Because young children have no firm concept about death, it seems to them that it is reversible. They may constantly ask when the dead child is going to return. Even older children who know that death is permanent may not respond to a sibling's death with a great show of emotion. One family was upset when their child went out to play right after the death of a sibling, and promptly had a serious fight with a neighbor's child. The parents were upset because he did not display grief, "but went wild fighting with the neighborhood children," not realizing that this was the child's way of releasing his feelings.

A sibling's normal behavior after the death may suddenly seem abnormal to the parents. This is not only because the child seems uncaring and unfeeling, but also because his normal rambunctiousness, misbehavior, and activity continue unabated. But a child's grief may be expressed in many different behaviors; among them regression, enuresis, nightmares, sullenness, somatic complaints, school phobia, withdrawal, hyperactivity, whining, crying, anorexia, or assuming the mannerisms of the dead sibling.

To some children, the death of a sibling means that the family can regroup, eat meals together, and do all the things illness prevented. It may seem perfectly harmless to an adolescent to say, "I'll be glad when Paine dies. Everybody is so miserable and he can't get better. We haven't been a family for so long we hardly know what it's like." Her parents may be deeply hurt, but they know exactly what the girl is saying and, in fact, they may feel the same way too.

Despite the parents' promise to return to normal or make up to the other children what they missed, the relationships between parents and children may never return to normal.

The alienation of family members may occur because children do not know how to behave around grieving parents. The "inappropriate" questions they ask may trigger the parents' anger. Similarly a child's dispassionate chatter about illness, injuries, anomalies, and death, which are his way of trying to grasp the reality of what has taken place, may be upsetting to his parents.

The parents' wish to protect the dead child's memory, or his or her sacrosanct possessions, not only postpones the return to normalcy but also deprives the surviving children of the love and attention they need. The survivors are angered at the enshrinement of a dead sibling, but still feel guilt about their anger. Secretly they may want to destroy or replace the pictures and memorabilia of the dead child, but this, too, causes uneasiness and guilt. In an attempt to take the place of the dead child, some siblings begin to emulate his life: join the same clubs, pursue the same interests, even make the same grades (whether good or bad) or develop the same mannerisms (ways of talking, walking, joking).

In other cases, siblings mature while parents are preoccupied with illness and grief, and succeed in establishing another life outside the home. It takes months, or even years, according to some parents, before they once again feel warmth and deep love for their other children—a fact which seldom escapes the attention of the children: "I know every time Mom hugs or kisses me she is thinking of my brother."

THE EFFECT OF ANNIVERSARIES

Anniversaries bring special memories. One sibling may try to give support to the parents, while another may carefully avoid saying anything that would remind the family of the sibling on the anniversary of the birth, death, or other significant event. Some children plan a treat or a special outing for their parents. Others write poems, tributes, or love notes to the dead sibling on his or her birthday. Diaries or notes of this kind are sometimes discovered years later by parents, who then realize for the first time how intense the sibling's love and grief were.

Chapter 6

Significant Others

This chapter focuses on two groups: the extended family, some of whom may be intimately involved in the life and death of the child, and those who are not related but whose lives are affected by the sickness and death of the child. In discussing these people, it becomes apparent that a great many people are affected by one child in the course of his or her short life.

All the people discussed in this chapter find themselves in a difficult and uncertain position during the illness and after the death. They do not want to impinge on the concerns of the immediate family, or add to the family's grief, or express their own grief in an inappropriate way.

The death of a child is a tragedy that no one in our society is prepared to accept as normal or reasonable. We think of death as inevitable only when the victim is old or in cases of serious incurable illness. Older relatives may express willingness to change places with a dying child to correct the injustice. "Why can't it be me? I've lived a full life. She hasn't begun." When disease or serious injury threaten a child, we turn to science and medicine, believing they must provide a cure.

Probably because the death seems so unfair and all efforts to support and console are either inappropriate or inadequate, many people who surround the family feel unable to help and are silenced by their grief.

GRANDPARENTS

A statement commonly made by pediatric staff (and even by parents themselves) is that grandparents are one of the biggest problems they have to cope with. Their most frequent transgressions are "butting in" and denying the accuracy of the diagnosis. Many parents find it necessary to reiterate constantly that the child will die. Typically the grandparents ask if all medical personnel are sure of the diagnosis. Citing instances in which patients whose condition was considered terminal rallied at the last minute and were eventually cured, they implore the parents to take their child to a well-known institution or a special physician, or to try a new drug or therapy. They assiduously read and clip stories from periodicals describing instances of misdiagnoses or miracle cures. Their purpose may be to legitimize their own denial, or else to manipulate the parents so that they are not the only ones to decide on the care and treatment of the child.

One family came to the clinic upset after receiving an article the grandmother had taken from a newspaper, which stated that the cancer their child had was contagious. In a note included with the clips the grandmother had written: "Watch those other children. How could you be so careless and uncaring as parents to let this contagious illness [not child] be around our grandchildren?"

In some cases, the staff may be told by the grandparents that they fear their children cannot cope. This may be a signal that the grandparents want to take over the care of the child. One grandparent asked that she, rather than the parents, be notified before any future decisions were made, because the parents, particularly the daughter-in-law, did not make decisions well.

When something tragic happens to their child, and their child's child, grandparents feel frustrated and helpless; they feel guilty about not knowing the answers and not being better able to cope. Instead of helping, they may find themselves accepting support from others, at a time when the "kids" need *their* support. Conversely, some grandparents feel lonely and angry because no one seems to recognize their pain. Their anger may be directed toward their child or grandchild, or at staff who do not appreciate all they do. This attitude is difficult for the staff to deal with. One grandparent talked steadily about her grief, so much so that the entire staff gave her more support than they gave the parents. After the death of her grandchild, several staff members came up to her and hugged *her* instead of going to the parents. The staff's confusion as to who needed the most support was apparent.

Grandparents who have been through the experience of losing a child themselves may indeed need more support, since they know the pain that their own child is going to face. Although they can empathize, they are often unable to give advice for fear of scaring the parents about all that lies ahead.

Grandparents feel they should set an example for their children and for all others involved in the crisis, yet they are frustrated by their inability to do so. In many cases, they experience guilt because they did not detect the symptoms of the illness or give better advice about the hazards of childhood accidents or of preventive medicine. A grandparent who helped care for the child before the diagnosis feels even more responsibility and guilt about the child's illness.

When a disease or anomaly is hereditary, guilt is experienced by the whole family. The grandparents are convinced that if they had been more careful, more inquisitive about the family's medical history the illness might have been prevented. When a young girl (an undiagnosed diabetic) died of ketoacidosis, the child's family denied any history of diabetes. The granparents, however, became upset about it because they did not know the cause of death of several relatives, any of whom may have been diabetic and passed on the disease.

An even more painful twist to the blame felt about hereditary disease occurs when one parent is discovered to be the carrier and is denounced by spouse or family. In one instance a mother-in-law told her daughter-in-law that the least she could do was continue caring for the child, then divorce her son so he could find happiness and another chance to have normal children.

Out of frustration, anger, and guilt, grandparents may become overprotective of the child and grandchild to the extent that they may forbid open discussion and/or punishment. When siblings want to talk about illness or death, they may be scolded for being insensitive or bad. Some grandparents go a step further and warn the siblings not to worry parents with questions.

Most parents have mixed feelings about treating their terminally ill child normally; constant criticism or conflicting advice from a parent or parent-in-law clouds the issue and makes it more difficult to decide on the child's best interests. Moreover, the grandparents may be consistently reassuring, or may continually correct the parents' gloomy reports with a more optimistic report of their own: "Things aren't nearly as serious as everyone lets on."

The Search for a Cause

In the search for a cause of the illness, previously suppressed hostilities between grandparents and their children or in-laws may come to the surface. Some grandparents complain about the housekeeping of their daughter or daughter-in-law, implying that a cleaner environment for the child would have meant better care and no disease. They may blame the couple because they both work and therefore have a full-time babysitter, believing that concerned parents would have been more vigilant.

In some cases it is apparent that the anger grandparents direct at the couple, the doctors, or whomever else, is a projection of their own guilt. Because it is easier to project than to face the blame, they attempt to resolve their guilt by conducting an intensive though futile search for the cause.

Only when a third party, perhaps a minister, or other relative, or staff member, intercedes can both sides vent their feelings in a constructive way. By carefully explaining the facts, and by allaying all the fears created by poor communication between parents and grandparents, a third party may help the family face the painful truth and develop more stable relationships.

MEMBERS OF THE EXTENDED FAMILY

The extended family consists of people directly related to the child. Such relatives find themselves excluded or powerless to help. They may simply rank among a great number of people who feel shattered at the impending loss of a child.

The extent of their grief will depend on the dynamics of the family and the strength of its emotional ties. Members of an extended family who live far apart may still feel close to each other, but may be able to regroup only at times of crisis. Between crises the family will turn to others for support.

Relatives who live in the same community as the parents of the dying child can give support in a number of significant ways, but primarily directly to the parents and child. Often the relatives can assist the family by acting as spokespersons, giving updated information to countless concerned people who hesitate to bother the family with constant telephone calls.

The impact of terminal illness on some relatives may differ little in intensity from that of the parents. In close families, aunts and uncles may be as fond of the child as his or her own parents, and the death represents a loss no less painful to them than the loss of one of their own children.

For the same reason, cousins may be as close as siblings, and when one cousin is suffering from a fatal illness, others may have problems similar to those of siblings. In one such instance, the staff gave permission for a child with a terminal illness to have his 13-year-old cousin stay with him in the hospital. The arrangement helped both the dying child and his cousin work through their grief by talking, joking, crying, and generally sharing their feelings. Largely as a result of this close relationship, the child was eventually able to talk freely to his parents and the sfaff.

BABYSITTERS

In families where both parents are employed as well as in one-parent families where the parent works, the babysitter frequently becomes like a member of the family. He or she sometimes becomes so attached to the children of the family that the conditions of employment are secondary to the affection for his or her "children." The babysitter may assume most of the responsibility for rearing the children.

Children often develop a relationship with their babysitter that differs little in closeness from that with the natural parents. The child's rapport with the babysitter may bring him comfort and mothering. In return he may call the babysitter "Mommy." In fact, some babysitters delight in the role of pushing the parents out and taking over.

Whether the babysitter stays with the children in the parents' home or is a friend of the family, neighbor, relative or licensed professional, if she cares for the children, she experiences the joys, headaches, accountability, and guilt of being a surrogate parent.

The full-time babysitter who cares for children at the time of the diagnosis invariably has the same reaction as the parents: She is smitten with guilt. Since she was given the responsibility of caring for the child, the sitter, like the parents, searches for a cause, or seeks to blame herself. Out of frustration, anger, or guilt, the parents may also blame the babysitter either directly or indirectly. Some parents charge that the babysitter wasn't doing her job if the child became sick or was injured while she was taking care of him. She should have recognized the symptoms. She was being paid to do that.

In other instances, the relationship between the babysitter and the parents deteriorates following the diagnosis, although not because of the parents' accusations. The babysitter may suddenly feel the responsibility of remaining is too great. The thought of caring for a child with a fatal disease is too frightening. Even when the child is in remission and in stable condition this problem may surface. In such cases, either together or separately, the babysitter and the parents need to confer with staff regarding her questions and fears.

The parents may decide as a result of diagnosis that they themselves must assume the responsibility of caring for the child rather than leave it to a babysitter. Guilt may force this decision. "Without us our child became ill. We didn't spend enough time with him." They want to make up all they think they and the child missed, and to spend the remaining time treasuring the child.

Almost without exception the babysitter believes she failed in her responsibility to the parents and child. It is all the more devastating if an infant dies at the babysitter's house from sudden infant death syndrome (SIDS) or by accident.

When the babysitter is taking care of more than one child and one of the children is a victim of SIDS or of an accident, other parents may become afraid to continue to employ the babysitter. The babysitter may concur:

You feel like a murderer. It all happens so suddenly and you can't believe it. You feel like taking on the responsibility makes you somehow special and protected from something like that happening. Then you're living it. Facing the parents is the worst thing of all. You have to tell them that the child who was fine when they left her is dead. I kept wishing I would die.

Similarly when the babysitter's own child dies, either as a result of an illness or suddenly and unexpectedly, the parents of other children may feel vulnerable.

She suddenly lost her baby two weeks ago. She started back sitting two days after the funeral. I know she's hurting, but I find myself scared. I feel guilty, but I get nervous thinking something may be around that my child could catch.

I know it was her child who was killed, but I think it happened once and it could happen again. You think people watch their own child closer than others. I wouldn't stop taking my child there. I think it'd make her feel more guilty. Several other parents have. You can see the hurt in her eyes. It's so awful.

When the babysitter is a relative, it may be too painful to express fears and doubts about whether she was attentive and careful enough. Yet the parent still has them. Even if parents reassure the babysitter that they do not blame her, she is not always sure whether they mean it or are just being kind.

In some cases the parents and the babysitter become closer after the diagnosis because of their shared concern for the child's welfare. Now more than ever before they must depend on each other. If the relationship is comfortable for both, they may be able to take turns during the long tense hours at the hospital so that the continuity in the child's care can be maintained by those whom the child trusts. This arrangement helps restore some of the normality of the parents' lives by allowing them time away from the hospital. One babysitter whose relationship with the family had always been friendly would periodically surprise the parents by telling them that they had an evening for themselves at no charge.

THE COMMUNITY

A lengthy terminal illness as well as the sudden unexpected death of a child has both an immediate and long-term impact on a large segment of the child's community. The child's short life may affect and touch hundreds of people either through personal contact, or indirectly when members of the community experience the tragedy vicariously.

A sense of community comes from common interests, from belonging to organizations and attending community functions. Many ties with the community are initiated by the children. Regardless of the size of the community, parent-teacher associations, scouting, sports competitions, church groups and the like provide a foundation for common interests and open avenues to communication and friendship.

At times of crisis and tragedy, families need fellow human beings who will give them support and empathize with them during grief. Community support may take many forms—transportation to the hospital, organized babysitting, help with the house and yard while the family is away, blood donations, fundraising drives, providing for the special needs of the child (e.g., donating books, records, a television set, radio, or tape recorder), or remembering the family with cards, letters, and telephone calls.

In a small community support may come from the population as a whole. It has been frequently observed that small communities resemble an extended family in closeness. In large cities, families may receive a different kind of support: the news of the family's plight and child's illness may be disseminated by the press or through the organizations that the child or family are connected with. Such organizations can be the source of financial or other kinds of support.

THE CHILD'S PEERS AND FRIENDS

A child's friends can be a great support during his illness. He may be dependent on them for the only intelligible description of what is going on in the world outside his hospital room or his home. Yet it becomes increasingly difficult for healthy children to share their lives—goals, achievements, activities in and out of school—with a child who is losing his life.

Fellow patients in the hospital become his peers. The child's former friends often feel rejected, fearful of saying or doing the wrong thing, or afraid of catching the same illness. Realizing how little they have in common as the disease process advances, they become reticent.

Nevertheless a child of any age enjoys receiving cards or telephone calls from classmates. Teachers of young school-age children can help by having the class write letters, design get-well cards, or schedule trips to the hospital (with the assistance of parents). Continued contact with peers and friends preserves the hope that the sick child and his friends will be reunited, which is very important to both school-age and adolescent children.

TEACHERS AND THE SCHOOL SITUATION

Handling the Terminally Ill Child

The title "teacher" makes one feel he or she should have all the answers. There are, however, no answers to the tragedy of terminal illness. Teachers cannot give them to students, the child, the family, or fellow teachers—least of all to themselves.

As authority figures facing many of the same problems parents encounter, teachers may also experience guilt in varying degrees for failing to observe the symptoms of disease or to prevent accidents. In some cases the teacher may be the first person to observe the symptoms and bring them to the attention of the family, which may, in turn, make the parents feel guilty about their "negligence."

Diagnosis of fatal illness inevitably alters the student's relationship with his or her teacher. Sudden favoritism toward a child who is not aware of her diagnosis may frighten her. Teachers' fears, like parents', are readily relayed to the child by a change in their attitudes.

The teachers' fears are expressed in questions, many of which are similar to those of the parents: What do I look for? What if he dies? What does "terminal" really mean? How normal is "normal?" How do I handle the parents? How strictly should attendance be enforced? How do I care for the child's special needs? What is the line between treating the child normally and giving special but appropriate considerations? What am I supposed to say to the child about the prospect of dying?

In rural schools a small student-to-teacher ratio often means a close relationship between students and teachers. The child who attends a rural or small school may be thought of as one of "my kids" by his teacher. In close relationships of this sort the teacher experiences deep grief when a terminal illness is diagnosed. When there are no special teaching programs or facilities to fall back on, the child's regular teacher may assume extra duties herself, on her own time, and thereby become part of the circle of intimates who constitute the child's only contact with the outside world.

In larger metropolitan schools the student's contact with each teacher may be restricted to a single class once a day. In the upper grades—junior and senior high school—the increased number of students under a teacher's control often precludes any personal association. Yet, when the child is ill or cannot attend classes, such school systems, because of their size, are often able to provide the best educational care.

The facilities available to help the student may be so numerous in such schools that they accomplish much the same thing as the community support system in smaller communities. Once they know of the illness, many of the child's teachers may drop in for a visit at the hospital or at home, often encouraging fellow students to do the same, or to call or write. Teachers in a large school system may find themselves as deeply involved in the personal tragedy of the dying child as their counterparts in smaller schools.

When the child returns to school after diagnosis, the overprotection he encounters can present problems for him and for those around him—peers, teachers, and parents. Some children take advantage of their illnesses at school, and for this reason it is important for parents to keep teachers informed about the illness, e.g., side effects of therapy, emotional stresses, behavioral changes, and remissions, so the teachers can adjust to the various changes. Teachers should have the freedom to call the parents and staff for updated information. Parents sometimes mistakenly believe that overprotection is in the child's best interest when, in fact, it simply hampers the teacher's efforts and prevents the child from performing well.

One child was ridiculed by her peers for wearing a wig. This became a problem for the teacher because he did not know why the child was wearing a wig or, consequently, how to handle the situation. When the teacher called the child's mother, the mother was evasive. The teacher began to fear the child might have an infectious illness that the mother was trying to conceal. Finally, after repeated problems at school and the child's persistent complaints to her mother, the mother called the teacher and explained that the wig was to cover temporary alopecia, a secondary effect of chemotherapy and radiation. The teacher explained the situation to the other pupils in the class. The child herself seemed pleased with the explanation and pulled her wig off to display her incoming hair.

Some parents, with the consent of their children, choose to conceal the diagnosis and hope for the best. A 16-year-old who began failing a chemistry course became upset and depressed. His mother, also quite upset, complained to the medical staff about the teacher. As it turned out, the mother had never informed the school about her son's diagnosis because she did not want "a nosey teacher prying or gossiping about him."

In most cases it is not a "nosey" teacher that a parent has to concern himself with, but an overprotective one. Frequently the overprotective teacher creates the disciplinary problem that the parents have been doing their best to avoid.

In general, overprotection subjects the child to ridicule and disfavor among peers. The extra attention does nothing more than emphasize the child's abnormality, and the rejection by peers strips away whatever normalcy there is in the child's life. School is to the child's social world what work is to the adult.

One adolescent girl asked hospital staff to talk to her teacher because from the time of diagnosis her homeroom teacher insisted on walking her from class to class. The girl, who had been in remission for over a year, was embarrassed by the attention; her friends were making fun of her, or ignoring her. Obviously, they were jealous and angry about the favoritism, which included not only a class-to-class faculty escort but also dispensation from homework and required projects, and high grades that were not deserved.

Certain compensations must be made when the child faces the problems of illness. He may be unable to participate in activities. He may need privacy to empty appliances or to take medication, or may require individualized attention to cope with the stresses of his illness. In general, the adjustment is less painful for the child if he is encouraged to be open about his problem. Teachers should give the child support and privacy, and supply factual information to classmates to satisfy their questions.

When compensations are made through favoritism or artificial excuses, students are resentful. One teacher got around this by having students volunteer to "help" her during recess. This practice proved to be very accommodating for a child in her class who had had radical surgery; the sick student was not left alone to feel useless. A school nurse invited a sick student to work as her assistant at a time when he was scheduled to go to gym class. "I know it better than her. I've lived it," said the student in recommending himself for the new assignment.

Occasionally a teacher goes to the opposite extreme to see that the child is treated normally — that is, she is stricter with the child than with his classmates. This often happens with children who suffer physical anomalies. However, many complaints of unfairness or even cruelty that parents make are based on a comparison with their own overprotectiveness.

The Problem of School Phobia

School phobia (i.e., fear of school) can be a common problem even when the child is in remission and doing well. Frequently it results from all the special attention he receives. His phobia may also be the result of worrying that something embarrassing might happen — such as vomiting in public, losing his wig, or being ridiculed by his classmates.

The terminally ill child, like the normal healthy child, must learn to face life and to fend for himself. When adults intercede to fight his fights, the child interprets their actions as proof of his inability to manage. He needs protection, therefore he is unacceptable to others, as the reasoning goes.

It made me so mad when my Mom yelled at those kids telling them they couldn't call me names. I was embarrassed. They'd yell, You can't walk right! Mom has to be your policeman! I hated to go to school or play after that. One day we were outside and the kids didn't want to play with me. I started to fight. Man, I really got hit, but I fought like fury. They knew that day no one was going to come running. The bruises felt good. It took a lot to calm Mom down, though. I told her I did it on purpose. After that I was back with the group. I wasn't afraid of school.

What passes for school phobia may, in some cases, be the parents' own separation anxiety. In a variety of ways the child's parents say, *don't go!* "What if you get sick?" "The kids may have something you'll catch." "What if you run a fever?" "What if the kids make fun of you?" "You haven't been away from home for that long." "You'll never catch up after all the work you've missed." The message "don't go" compels some children to remain in the protective shell of home. Or, after some encouragement, the child may venture out only to prove the parent right: "I knew I would throw up." "The kids did make fun of me." "I'll never be able to catch up."

Some teachers of terminally ill children may be relieved when the child does not return for whatever reason. They no longer have to worry about the child, or fear what will happen when he is in their care.

Following diagnosis, some children announce that they will not return to school. The anguish over the diagnosis is somewhat lessened by the satisfaction of not going back to school. In some cases, this is the child's way of manipulating his parents, using the illness as an excuse to avoid going to school or doing anything he does not want to do. Therefore the likelihood of school phobia should be anticipated at the time of diagnosis so that it can be avoided, if possible.

If they lack appropriate information, school administrators may not know that the child is able to attend school. Some families wait, or think they are waiting, for doctors to tell them when the child can return to school. Months may go by while the child is lounging around home, watching daytime television, usually thoroughly bored.

Hospital Schools

The child may be physically ill and incapacitated but his mind requires nourishment and stimulation. Hospital schools can help satisfy these needs. When a child who has attended hospital school returns to regular school after his release from the hospital, the difficult chore of catching up will be less onerous. Not all hospitals provide schooling despite its importance to a child who is admitted for extended periods.

Hospitals schools allow the child time away from the medical environment. Younger children are usually enthusiastic about the program; hospitalizations seems less traumatic to them when they can look forward to school. Older children may complain that hospital school is less stimulating, often with good reason; the mix of age groups and the range of health problems among those in the classroom can be distracting and make learning difficult.

A 10-year-old girl who was in an accelerated program announced one day that she would not return to her class because a retarded child had been yelling, another child had vomited, and a third was disruptive. In cases like this, the hospital school should be flexible enough to make allowances for the bright student as well as the handicapped student.

There are a number of ways in which children can continue their education when they are physically unable to be present in the classroom on a regular basis. Arrangements can be made in public or private schools for children to attend selected classes, participate in special activities, or attend a favorite class.

Children who are homebound from the time of diagnosis, or periodically throughout their illness, can often avail themselves of special homebound programs to keep pace with classmates and continue living with some semblance of normalcy. Homebound teaching provides a form of contact with the outside world other than contact with relatives and medical staff. The most successful and beneficial programs are those that provide incentive to excel; when there are tests and deadlines for work, success brings a real sense of achievement.

Audio homebound, where it is available, allows the child to be part of his regular class by giving the same instruction by a special telephone or visual hookup.

OTHER SCHOOL PERSONNEL

The School Nurse

The concern of the school nurse is health care, and she may be the logical person to act as liaison between the family and the school. She may also be the resident source of medical information for students and faculty. To the faculty she can provide updated information on the child's condition. Her experience enables her to cooperate with the medical and behavioral problems.

A child who was comfortable discussing his illness with hospital nurses may prefer to confide in the school nurse rather than teachers or counselors, feeling a similar comfort in discussing with her his fears and the situations he has to deal with.

One 13-year-old boy who was in remission spent much of his time in the school nurse's office. His complaints were vague although it was no secret that he was teased by classmates about his weight gain (cushingoid effects) and alopecia secondary to vincristine. He worried greatly about his body image, peer relationships, prognosis, family problems, and the increasing pressure from his father to strive for perfection. The school nurse kept the medical team informed of the problems. In return, the medical team provided a great deal of support for her and the rest of the faculty, which was helpful in her continuing dialogue with the child.

School Counselors

The concerns and anxieties of ill students of any age are real and should be treated with respect and consideration. For example, students may feel uncomfortable facing their teachers daily after unburdening themselves of some very privileged information. Such experiences may also affect how teachers relate to the student and thus may require the intervention of the school counselor.

Because students often regard counselors as being distinct from the faculty, some of them find it easier to talk to counselors than to their teachers.

School Personnel Can Help with Communication

Teachers, school nurses, and counselors all occupy positions of respect in the community as well as at school, which enables them to obtain and disseminate information pertaining to the dying child. The insight of each and the interaction of all can be invaluable in dealing with the problems of the dying child or in eliciting proper responses from the child's classmates.

Confidentiality is vital to relationships with the dying child. At times, however, the information imparted needs to be given to the proper sources, for example, suicide threats, signs of relapse, or severe family problems. The child should be encouraged in such cases to talk with another professional, someone in his family, or a member of the medical team. In some instances, children will ask that the teacher, school nurse, or counselor accompany them to help articulate their problems.

EMPLOYERS OF THE PARENTS

Most employers are understanding during the acute stresses of terminal illness, but, as in the case of friends and relatives, their desire to help, which is stong at the beginning, often decreases during the fluctuations of illness. An employer's understanding may be tested to the limit by the employee's frequent, unexpected leaves, continual absences, daydreaming, accidents, preoccupation, or inefficiency. The employees themselves may be disturbed by these lapses, unavoidable as they are, knowing that poor performance may jeopardize that job.

Many employers respond to the parent's needs with kindness and generosity. For example, they may make it possible for the parent to get off work, often without a loss of pay; promote fund-raising drives to help with medical expenses; round up blood donors; give bonuses so the family can take a vacation or allow the parent a leave of absence; or provide the use of a telephone so the parent can call the hospital or the doctor for daily reports.

An employer may fall into the common pattern of trying to shelter the employee in the beginning. The consequence of preferential treatment may be to heap more work on fellow employees, thereby prompting their resentment.

Employers are apt to experience a vague sense of guilt in addition to pity. They may have little understanding of the disease process and, unless otherwise informed, may wonder whether the child was really all that sick when he or she is released from the hospital. Some parents do not want to give an employer the opportunity to pity them or give them special treatment and so they minimize the seriousness of the child's illness. The employer then feels guilty when he or she finds out the child is critically ill or has died, believing that the employee could have been given more support.

Fellow employees often have a difficult time dealing with a coworker after the diagnosis, first because they can easily project the impact on their own lives, and second because they fear contagion. They, too, should be given adequate and correct information either by the parent, a relative, a reliable friend, or by a member of the health care team.

The Problem of Job Security

It frequently happens that during prolonged illness a parent must wrestle with the decision of whether to leave the security of one job for a potentially more promising one. The parent worries not only about financial risks or about losing health insurance, but also about the consequences such a move might have on the child's overall health care. Hospital staff may be able to answer some questions, but because there are so many unknowns, a parent will no doubt be forced to remain in a job until the child dies.

In an extreme instance of this predicament, one father found himself at the mercy of an employer with severe emotional problems. Because the group insurance plan was generous, the father said, after the diagnosis, "I was stuck with the job." The boss would threaten to fire the father whenever it pleased him: "You're stuck with it and you know it. Now you'll do what I want *when* I want." (This statement was verified by fellow employees who were in contact with hospital staff.) The morning the child died the employer refused to let the boy's father go to the hospital. Throughout the ordeal and for months after the child's death, the father was forced to stay with the company to meet his financial obligations.

EMPLOYERS OF THE TERMINALLY ILL

An employer who has terminally ill adolescents working for him is plagued by the same concerns as the child's parents, babysitters, or teachers: What to do if something goes wrong? Frequently such fears do not go unnoticed by the child, and to prove his normalcy, an adolescent will perform the most difficult jobs. Rather than satisfying the employer that everything is all right, a demonstration of this sort usually has the opposite effect: increased apprehension because the child is pushing himself too hard.

Legal complications can be a significant risk for employees, but most take that risk because of the responsibility they feel toward the dying child. For the young person, the salary earned means accomplishment and independence. To himself and others, his job proves he can carry on with life even though the time is short. Many youths are forced to lie about their diagnosis in order to get a job. This is particularly true of youngsters who work their way through school or have family responsibilities.

Without a clear understanding of the disease process, an employer may live from minute to minute in fear that the child will die. In fact she may be so fearful that the terminally ill employee will die on the job that she may encourage him to quit. One boss listed all the things that needed doing, then pared down the list to almost nothing by eliminating things he felt would be too much for the youth. The employee's response was, "You know, I'm not going to die in front of you. My disease is in control."

FELLOW PARENTS

The familiar notion that "no one understands unless he has been through it" is true when applied to the agonizing course of a child's terminal illness. Parents in similar situations provide a pool of strength that few counselors, psychologists, or other members of the health care team can match. Fellow parents derive courage from observing one another, and recognizing each other's strengths and weaknesses. Fellow parents can set the example for modes of coping, defining which ones are appropriate.

Parents are brought together in the most awkward social setting: in waiting rooms, during medical procedures, in bathrooms, halls, and stairwells. They have a pressing need to find out from other parents how to cope, how to get by.

Parents discuss every aspect of their children—age, sex, intelligence, looks—and of their feelings toward them. They talk about their own fears and frustrations, their relations with staff, and, above all, their pain. Sharing their feelings openly with other parents assures them of their normalcy or else helps them discover they have special problems to be worked out.

They compare therapies and their children's responses to them, possibly to discover why their own child's therapy is different from that of another. Will the child's response to therapy be the same or better or worse than another child's? Will their child go through the same cycle as another? They discuss what their child may look like in the future. They see children who cannot walk or talk, those who are in pain, those frequently admitted, those in remission, those unable to attain remission and, occasionally, those cured. They see what their life has been and what it will be. "I guess you'd say we share hope that is hopeless. It's the only thing that keeps us going."

They pump each other for facts or clues that might explain the disease or make the child's course easier. They search for the similarities and the differences that may unlock the meaning of the child's fate. All these exchanges help parents to face up to the outcome of the ordeal they are going through, an ordeal that has the texture of a bad dream.

Parents frequently ask the staff about other parents or other children rather than asking those parents directly, for fear the news will be bad. Even when their own child is in the terminal phase, they may ask timidly if other parents whose children are also in the terminal phase have stopped therapy. Some parents who are opposed to a lingering death for their child take no steps to avoid it for fear of being judged different.

It is common for parents to ask how other parents are doing at similar stages of their child's illness so they can compare their own state of mind and assess their own reserves for whatever lies ahead. In testing the staff by their questions ("How is so and so doing?") they are really asking, and in their own minds assessing, "How am I doing?" "How should I be doing?" or "How will I do?"

Parents become keen observers of one another, as well as of the staff. They watch newly diagnosed parents begin their grieving process in shock and disbelief, and relive what they have already experienced. They watch as the child's belongings are piled on a cart to be taken home, and they watch the parents' befuddled movements before they leave for the last time.

They become accustomed to the reality of their child's diagnosis and they make the preliminary adjustment to the child's impending death. In many cases, they talk frankly in front of their child about other children's illness and death. Inevitably their fears mount when they see children who are experiencing complications or who are in the terminal phase.

Fellow parents' sensitivity to the needs of others has its limits. At times they feel too drained to listen to another parent's problems. Typically, parents are intolerant of others who keep saying they have total control of themselves when, as everyone knows, they do not. They are apt to have little patience with parents who chatter continually, but avoid talking about their true feelings. Fellow parents who use their child's disease to gain sympathy or special treatment are usually ostracized.

At times, they see other parents whose child does not have an incurable illness go to pieces over a minor surgical or other procedure. They are naturally unsympathetic to such reactions, or to parents' complaints about school starting, vacation problems, or other trivial events, because they know their own child will never again engage in normal activities.

PARENT SUPPORT SYSTEMS

In the absence of a formal group directed by professionals to help parents resolve questions, problems, and grief, parents may spontaneously develop their own support system. Because parents share their need for support more readily with fellow parents than with staff members, professional supervision is not essential. Support is almost automatic at critical times, or when a child is dying.

Couples worry about the parents without spouses, knowing how lonely their lives can be. They tend to give more support to others who are in more distress than themselves, such as parents of recently diagnosed or relapsed children. It is extremely frightening for the parents of newly diagnosed children to meet the children who are terminal. The experience is equivalent to moving themselves and their child forward in time to that dreaded moment. Sensing this, other parents whose children are far advanced provide hope: "I wish I were in your place with all the research being done and the new therapies. You have more hope than we did at the beginning."

Parents usually arrive at the point where they feel more comfortable with other parents in the same situation than with relatives or friends. Prejudices vanish amid the stresses of their lives. Parents form a group that allows openness and accepts the insecurities and fears of its members. Illness becomes the whole focus of their existence.

In some cases, families remain in contact after the death of one of the children in the group. Cards, letters, and telephone calls can be extremely supportive, but the disparity in situtations puts a strain on both sides. The family who lost the child may be glad that their ordeal is over, but they are nevertheless jealous about the survival of another child.

> I feel so inhuman because I have no feelings. I'm so bitter over my own child there's nothing left for others. I feel so guilty.

> I see now what some of these children and their families are going through and I'm glad we didn't have to face all that. At the time I was angry and prayed mine would live. Little did I know what I was praying for.

The parent whose child survives feels a strange hesitancy to share his good fortune; he may feel guilty because his child is doing well or, even if she is doing poorly, still surviving. Only fellow parents can understand and be glad that their terminally ill child is better off than another child who is also terminally ill.

The survivors have both the privilege and pain of treasuring every moment. And there is always hope in the moment. The parents whose children have died have lost the moment with their child. It is difficult to understand the survivors' disproportionate gratitude until one realizes how they look at their situation: temporarily they have something priceless that other parents do not have.

THE CHILD'S FELLOW PATIENTS

Just as parents derive a great deal of support from fellow parents, pediatric patients get help from one another. This is particularly true of older school-age and adolescent patients, but young patients, too, show concern for one another. At any age, however, the support they give to someone else is not generally put into words. They fear what is happening to fellow patients as well as what lies ahead for them. Even during remission, the fear does not go away.

Children are proud of themselves when they can be supportive of other patients. If no one on the staff or in the family has experienced surgery, alopecia, side effects from therapy, disfiguring injuries, and so on, only a fellow patient in a similar situation can tell a new patient what it is like. The special role of helping another reach a more comfortable state of mind gives the young patient status and dignity.

Like their parents, children compare procedures, therapy, diagnoses, the course of their illness, reactions to and from staff, family, and others. If allowed, children often ask about the diagnosis of fellow patients: "What does the new kid have? Has he ever been here before? Does he know what he had?" They receive an immense amount of information by watching and listening and being around other patients. Hence they grow up fast from experiencing their own illness and that of other patients.

Children are concerned about fellow patients, particularly when they are at the same stage in their illnesses. They feel lucky when they do not have to go through what a fellow patient undergoes, yet the awareness of another's suffering is also painful. The concerned child worries not only about friends but about himself and what is in store for him.

> I hate to see George go through all that new chemotherapy. It makes him so sick. We have done the same in our disease until now. He's such a nice guy to have to be so sick.

The child's concern is no less than his parents' when he learns that another child who is ahead of him in the disease processs no longer comes to the clinic. The child's absence may mean that some other activity took precedence, but it may also be the result of hospitalization, relapse, or even death.

The Death of a Fellow Patient

Children react to deterioration and deaths in other patients in different ways. A preschooler whose friend died of an illness similar to his began having stomachaches following his friend's death. The stomachaches stopped after he talked with his parents about the death, his anger, and the loss he felt. He cried with his his parents and afterward said, "I don't think I have to hurt any more. It's all been taken away." Another preschooler, depressed after the death of her close friend, insisted on visiting the clinic and seeing all the patients. It appeared she had to convince herself that not all her friends had died. After the visit she announced, with some relief, "I guess they're doing okay. Now let's go and have fun."

The older child may become moody, or even suspend all communication after the death of a friend. Other reactions to a loss include enuresis, withdrawal, regression, and temper tantrums.

Fellow patients can become angry and frustrated when they find out that other patients have died and they have not been told.

> I knew Thorp died. I just wanted to hear how everybody reacted. Some really became nervous, especially the doctors. Others pretended not to hear. They cut me off like I said something bad. Some just stood there looking sad. Some didn't say anything. They looked like they wanted to die rather than talk about it.

Many children probe for more information when they are allowed to talk about a friend's death. What were the parents' reactions? Will they be all right? how was the funeral? Did the staff react? Does everyone cry? Will they get fired if they cry? What did the child look like? Was the child scared or hurting? Children need to talk about the death of a fellow patient because it helps them adjust to their own impending death. Some may even attend the funeral of fellow patients. They are angered when, at the time of death, they are shifted from their room to another, or even diverted to another floor, so they do not see the child's family leaving the hospital for the last time. Parents' natural inclination is to gather with fellow parents after the death of a child. Children wish to do the same. A nurse may observe patients huddled together discussing "private matters." After such discussions the children look relieved. "I knew Jennie died and I had to talk to someone. It really helped to have someone who knew what it was all about to talk with."

When children are not allowed to talk about their own illness and death, they may find some relief in recounting the experiences of other patients. In some cases, their unintentional slips reveal who they are really talking about:

> My roommate really cried the night he was told there wasn't a cure for his disease. We talked most of the night. I knew what he was going through. He kept saying it wasn't fair that he had to go through it. I really . . . I mean, he really got mad at having to face all the crap.

Talking about another person may be the only way children have of communicating their feelings. It may be acceptable to adults for children to talk about fellow patients, but not for them to reveal their own feelings.

THE HEALTH CARE TEAM

It is natural for the medical team who becomes involved with the child and the family after the diagnosis, and maintains close contact throughout the course of illness, to develop a strong emotional attachment to them. But other personnel who have far less direct contact with child and family are also drawn into the tragedy. Families often find support coming from people throughout the hospital.

For example, technicians who seemingly work behind the scenes, performing numerous different functions in caring for the dying child, may become interested in the child as a person and not just as a statistic or a unique case.

This is as it should be. Total care extends beyond the confines of the physician's office, the hospital, or the clinic. The staff has the responsibility to prepare the family for what lies ahead as well as to assist them in handling the daily stresses that spring from their child's terminal illness. Although it is impossible for all the staff to become directly involved, much can be accomplished through education of the child and family, and nonjudgmental listening and counseling. In some cases, it is only through helping the family that staff members can cope with their own grief.

Hospital Staff

> After the death of a child, I treasure so many things. It is through these children that I have changed my values in life so drastically. You can't work with grief without your life being changed. Some people change to bitterness. I have those feelings sometimes, but, in general, I have a more positive attitude about life. I know it is totally unfair, but I have learned to treasure the moment and people more because of others' pain.

The care of dying children is extremely demanding both physically and emotionally. The staff discover they are not superhuman even though the role and the responsibilities often seem to require it. Their emotional involvement with the child and his or her family makes them vulnerable to intense grief.

The stages of grief the staff experience may not correspond with those the family is going through, nor is their grief as deep; but the constant exposure to chronic grief is a great strain. The care of dying children requires emotional stability as well as technical skills. It should be pointed out that little emotional support is offered to these professionals. The tendency is to assume that one becomes experienced with and also immune to grief as a result of continual care of dying children. The only support from people in and out of the profession may be the advice to "get out of it if it upsets you."

Staff members find numerous defenses to help them cope with the stresses of their occupation. The most common is intellectualization, which implies a rational approach to the problems, precluding emotions. It is successful only when one's feelings can be suppressed. One can hide behind a uniform, a title, a degree, or medical terminology only so long before facing the reality of the human situation. At best the professional masters the appearance of calm, disguising pain and fear.

The professional, like the family, tries to bargain—to look for hopeful outcomes to an essentially hopeless situation: more time, new research, new therapy, unexpected changes or responses in the patient. The professional is aware of all the knowledge available in the field, but also knows the limitations. Frequently this realization leads to more bargaining: "I often think after the hours I spend with the family and child that things should go better." "All my education and experience should be compensated somehow."

The objectives of the health care profession, and medicine in particular, are prevention and cure. Palliation and death are incompatible with these ideal goals. When medical personnel are faced with the diagnosis of incurable illness, their professionalism, expertise, and knowledge may all seem pitifully inadequate. This is particularly true when the diagnosed child's parent is a doctor or nurse.

> You know so much it scares you, but, at the same time, you feel a type of immunity from it happening to you. It's always somebody else. When a doctor's or nurse's child comes in, I think, My God! We're not safe either. It's like if I think about it, it can't possibly happen to me.

Medical personnel, in many cases, feel the failure not only professionally but also personally. Ironically, the health care profession, whose goal is to prolong life, is filled with people who are supposedly experts on death and dying. Health care professionals are often plagued with fears and insecurities about death and dying because their orientation is toward lengthening and saving life. To adjust to the inevitability of so many deaths is somehow to compromise one's performance, they feel. No matter what their experience with death and grief, to a professional each death is unique.

Handling the Diagnosis

The most painful aspect of medicine is telling a family that one of its members is dying. The pain is compounded when the dying one is a child. Some families want to know what lies ahead. Even if they could be predicted accurately, a description of the nightmarish experiences in store would be too upsetting to the family at the outset.

> I'm glad they don't know what's ahead. They are grieving now, but they have hope. They gradually realize the horror of it all. I see those cute kids come in and I can picture what they will go through. I really get depressed. It's all so unfair. My heart aches for the hope these families have. They often think the medical center is a Mecca, and we have a cure for anything.
>
> I get more depressed at the time of diagnosis, relapses, and the terminal period

than I do at the death of the child. His suffering and the parents' anticipation are over. I realize the family has the intense grief to face, but they don't have the constant fears of living daily with the unknown terror of when, where, and how it will end.

Knowing the approximate sequence of events that lie ahead for the child and family might seem to make it easier for the staff to adjust, but it does not. The prospect of death is no more acceptable to the staff dealing with hemopoietic deviations, for example, than to the staff in high-risk units such as emergency rooms, neonatal intensive care, or burn centers. Both face constant grief: acute, anticipatory, chronic. Nevertheless, some staffs are more adept than others at dealing with the children and the families. They regard the inevitability of death not as a failure, but as a challenge to make the child's remaining time more meaningful.

Facing Guilt and Frustration

The staff who deal with dying children are frequently afflicted with guilt. They worry if they have done everything correctly and everything possible. Did they hurt the child unnecessarily? Did they order enough tests or too many? Could they have prevented problems or complications? They feel guilty over their failures, inability to hide emotions, to answer questions, support or communicate with the child, and so on.

One nurse who had given a child chemotherapy throughout his illness had difficulty with the venipuncture two days before his death. The child cried and screamed, and another staff member eventually gave the chemotherapy.

I was so depressed I went home and cried. I don't think he realized how painful that was for me. We were so close. I knew he was terminal, but I didn't think he would die that soon. That keeps haunting me — his crying and begging me to stop hurting him. We always had a lot of fun before, even with the pain. That was our last interaction.

As might be expected, tempers became short, dissatisfaction rife, and morale low if staff are faced with many deaths at one time or in one unit.

You feel you have to play the brave role for the parents and other patients. When there have been several deaths or many who are terminal, everybody gets depressed, angry, and guilty. Some deny that their favorite kids are dying. You feel like you have no answer. The "why" is always there. Families ask it, and I ask it as much, if not more, than they do because I see so many children dying. When you share your feelings with others, they often advise you to work in another area. They don't realize you may love your work, the kids, and the families. You just need to grieve.

The staff represents not only hope but failure. Frequently staff members vent their anger—a product of their own frustration—by lashing out at someone else. The anger may be directed at pharmacy, which has delayed the delivery of a prescription, a medical student who is not adept, central service for being out of some needed equipment, housekeeping, the page operator, or a fellow driver on the way home.

Each stage of grief the patient and family experience has its own frustrations for the staff. The staff may be frustrated at the family's refusal to admit that their child is dying, but also are mystified by the staff physician who is ordering measures that appear equally unrealistic.

When treatment becomes palliative, the staff feel frustration and anger not only because of the child and his family but also at their own limitations and their inability to control such a painful situation. It can be excruciating to learn from parents that a child awoke *only* five times during the night or that her pain medication helped her for a *whole* hour.

> I feel so guilty and helpless when a parent thanks me for helping their child be without pain. You're doing something, yet you feel helpless, angry, and guilty. It's not fair. No 2-year-old, 5-year-old, 10-year-old, or 16-year-old should have to have pain medications to exist. It isn't even living.

Abandonment by Staff

In spite of the closeness and affection the staff may develop for patient and family, they may emotionally abandon them at some stage of the illness. "They [the family] won't talk anymore. It doesn't do any good to talk to them because they're angry. They're unreachable. They are pulling away. They want to be left alone." Dealing with the family and the child is avoided by using such pretenses. Rounds may become noticeably shorter as death approaches, and lights may be answered less promptly.

Some staff members are perfectly aware of the abandonment but are utterly powerless to prevent it. "I know I'm pulling away, and I feel terrible about it, but I can't help it. I'm not sure who I'm protecting. Myself? The child and family?"

In other instances there is no admission of guilt, merely a desperate retreat. One nurse expressed her dissatisfaction with a physician who abandoned a family, leaving nurses and students to face the problems. A child was obviously dying, but when the parents asked about her, the physician stated she was terminal but might last several days. He advised the family that he would clarify his remarks the following morning. After he left the child's room he told the resident that the child would not survive the night. "He ran from the situation, yet he is in that specialty," the nurse commented. "The parents felt bad because their child died before the physician had predicted she would. He also said he would be home if the parents wanted to talk, or wished him to return. We called all evening. There was no answer. I hate not only the running but the lying."

The Sense of Loss

The sense of loss staff members feel at the time of diagnosis, relapse, or death may intensify the affection they feel for their own children.

> You appreciate your own children more. The messiness doesn't drive me as crazy as it used to. I just think of those parents wishing they had those messy little hands around. You treasure the time with your children more. The trips to the zoo and picnics are more important than making sure the house is clean. You find yourself thinking, "What if I were in those parents' shoes?" I know I'd go crazy. I'd be a basket case.

At the same time pathology can become an obsession.

> You have to be really careful not to make every bruise leukemia, every bump a tumor, every cough a five-lobed pneumonia, every shortness of breath a cardiac anomaly.

Worrying about one's own child, yet being intolerant of the child's complaints, is a common reaction to blocking out the experience of work so one can enjoy home life.

The staff express a sense of loss in many ways. The staff physician may be quieter, moodier than usual, more demanding. A staff nurse may become more critical of the care given to patients, and less tolerant of fellow patients and families. Families are not always aware of the acute impact death and dying have on the staff.

> I know they think we go along with our work and don't think about it. We feel we have to do that for the other families. If you know the staff you can sense the feelings loud and clear. You can tell it in their behavior. Pain permeates the atmosphere.

One staff member kept a scrapbook of the children. One day she was cleaning when she found the book. She began looking through it and found the pictures, many of them showing the children at various stages of their illnesses. "You don't realize how special each of those children is," she said. "I cried for several hours. I think I had held in that grief for a long time. Sometimes you have to go through it alone."

Frequently some association will bring back memories of the child: a certain perfume, a television program, a commercial, a joke, an ice cream flavor, a movie. Several years after the death of one child some staff members admitted to one another that none of them could stand the smell of lilies because it brought back memories of that particular child. The child died on Good Friday and 2 days before his death the family brought him a lily.

Another staff member reported being in a grocery store the day after one of her special children died.

His favorite commercial came on. I stood there crying and laughing at the same time. People looked at me like I was nuts. One woman came over and asked if there was anything she could do. I don't think you could understand, I told her. It was like he was really there. I think with incidents like that, I can partially understand what the families go through.

It is as important for staff to be open as it is for the patient and family. Formal and informal groups can be a tremendous help. Staff who are more experienced with the grief process can provide an atmosphere of acceptance and warmth and serve as role models for the expression of grief.

After the Death

The decision whether to attend the funeral or visit the funeral home is made with the utmost difficulty. The fear that one's appearance may cause the family to relive the experience of suffering and pain may be sufficient incentive to abandon the idea; families report, however, that important people in their child's life still mean a lot to them. The appearance of a staff member at the funeral proves to the family how much the child meant to the staff.

Visiting the funeral home or attending the funeral are, in many cases, necessary steps in working through one's own grief.

It cements the reality of their death. When I don't see them dead, I find myself denying that it happened. That sounds horrible, I'm sure. It has happened with some of my favorite children. I find myself still expecting them to return to the hospital.

After the death, the link that joined the families and staff disappears, like the one between parents whose children are surviving and those who have begun postdeath grief. When families visit the unit following the death of their child, it is not uncommon for them to find staff members extremely ill at ease. Despite the long-standing comfortable relations, all involved act like strangers. Conversation is sporadic and awkward. Yet later, in a more relaxed moment, the staff may look back on the family's visit with satisfaction. It showed that the family cared enough to return. "These visits are usually painful. Some more than others. It helps me resolve my grief, however. Also I know how the family is doing then."

Staff members are often worried about the propriety of home visits. The decision of whether or not to continue such visits has to be an individual one. In general, it should be noted that at least one visit is usually beneficial for both sides.

It helps to know the family still wants you to visit. They talk more when they are in their own home. We can grieve together. It is the place where most of the memories are, both good and bad. It's more appropriate there.

HOW MINISTERS DEAL WITH GRIEF

Minister: You must accept the will of God.
Mother: Is His will for Nick to die? I just don't buy that. I don't care what
            you say. I love my son. I don't want him to die. I can't accept it.
Minister: I can't either.

The traditional view of the minister is of one who is less vulnerable to human feelings because of his overriding concerns with spiritual matters. Only recently, in fact, have schools of theology felt the need to include courses in the psychological aspects of the grief process.

The common notion that ministers are pious and aloof often prevents them from living up to all the demands of society. The display of emotions, for instance, may be taken as a sign that their faith is weakening. Yet the minister who is summoned to the hospital to provide counsel to the family of a terminally ill child may not feel like preaching or instructing. The bereaved family who says, "It isn't fair," may be surprised by the sympathetic response from the minister.

People look to a minister for answers at a time when he himself is evaluating the loss. He may have close emotional ties with the family or he may be the father of a child of the same age as the one he buried. Suddenly he is unable to find anything remotely comforting to say, for all his knowledge and training.

Some ministers believe that the prayers and religious explanations required of them offer a consolation, despite their own grief and anger at the time. But having complied with their obligation they still have to deal with their own human feelings and their own need for answers.

Some families tentatively accept religion during their child's illness in the hope that a cure will be offered in exchange. In some instances, ministers encourage a religious experience for just this reason. But when no cure is forthcoming or when exacerbation occurs, the family, in its anger, may repudiate the faith.

One family who turned to a faith healer after their own religion "failed" them became less and less able to accept the reality of the child's disease. During one of the faith healer's visits he was overheard telling the child and the parents that the disease was cured, and that the staff was lying about the illness. The proof of the miracle would be the family's faith. If they kept the faith then all would go well and the child could return to a normal life. The child was in the terminal phase of his illness. For days the family rejected the fact that the child was ill. When the child's death was imminent and could no longer be denied, the parents became severely depressed.

Ministers as Parents

The minister who has a child diagnosed as having a terminal illness, or one who dies suddenly and unexpectedly, often finds himself without emotional support. This is usually the case when he and his family feel they should play the role of accepting Christians. Anger, shock, depression, and guilt are normal feelings for any parent. But for a minister, anger toward God may be irreconcilable with his beliefs.

The support that comes from community, family, and friends (including fellow ministers and their families) is quite often different from the support offered to lay families in a crisis. A common misconception is that the minister does not fear death as the rest of the world does. The minister himself may work hard to leave this impression.

One minister whose child was terminally ill would loudly proclaim for the child's benefit and for others within earshot: "How happy we are that Rad is going to heaven soon. There he will be, an angel, happy forever." All efforts to encourage the father to express his grief were blunted: "You don't know what it's like to be a man of God, happy that God has chosen your child for an angel." The child's uncontrollable behavior, and the family's obvious depression and inability to become part of a parent group resulted in tension between this family and other families and staff.

Considered the most knowledgeable of men on the subjects of faith and hope, ministers are often left to face travail alone. One minister's wife said, in a moment of despair, "I wish we hadn't so much faith. Then I could be human." People had been telling the couple how "lucky" they were to be so special and to have such strong faith because this would make their experience bearable.

> Now I know what it's like and it's horrible. I wouldn't say that to anyone, especially my husband. I know he's hurting badly, but he'd never share it. All his friends are so joyful and don't allow us to talk about Sol. We have to withdraw, smile and be happy that God is so good to us. I'm sick of the role. I want to yell and scream that I hate this, but I don't.

A footnote to this story is that the mother never again allowed herself to confide in the staff. At one point she said, "Forgive my weakness at that time. I have prayed and am most peaceful now. My husband says we must accept it cheerfully and I am."

In an altogether different situation a father and minister cried openly after his child was diagnosed with a terminal illness. He and the family received abundant support from the staff, fellow parents, other ministers, and the hospital chaplains. The man also became very close to his parishioners because of the experience. Fellow parents felt a close bond because he had shown his humanness.

THE ROLE OF HOSPITAL CHAPLAINS

In a large medical center the hospital chaplain often finds himself wearing the vestments of many religious leaders. Chaplains freely admit they are adaptable: "For one person I'm a Methodist, for another I'm a Baptist, or Catholic, or Unitarian, or Jew." Because of the distance some families must travel from the home community, the hospital chaplain is often expected to substitute for the family minister.

The chaplain is usually unfamiliar with the patient's and family's coping mechanisms. Many chaplains worry about families with whom they have brief contact during a crisis, and who are then sent home to face the intense grief of their loss. Some write or call after the death to provide support and assess the family's progress; but the support they provide is limited, and this seems to run contrary to their calling. In cases where a family from a distant community remains at the hospital, the chaplain can serve as a liaison between the family minister and the parents of the sick child.

Families and patients need the assurance that the hospital chaplain is always at hand and can be called when they need him. They also need reassurances that the minister's visit does not necessarily imply that the end is near even when the staff summon the chaplain without the family's requesting it. The family should be informed that the staff will call for the chaplain when they deem it necessary for the family's well-being.

In some instances, families feel abandoned by their own minister who is unable to visit. The hospital chaplain often assumes the role their family minister is unable or unwilling to fill. The family needs support throughout the illness, not just during the terminal period or at death. Some parents who tell their minister about the child's diagnosis are embittered by the minister's lack of support throughout the course of illness. "We needed him for support all along, not just to bury our child."

MEDICAL AND NURSING STUDENTS

In large medical centers students account for a large proportion of the medical team. Even in small community hospitals, student nurses and residents often moonlight or rotate on a preceptorship with physicians. As the newest members of the team, their freshest lessons are often blunted by their experiences with death and dying.

Typically students find it extremely difficult to work with death because death seems contrary to what they have been taught. They may come away confused and frightened from an experience of working with the child and family. Students find it difficult, even threatening, to care for dying children, even though their youth is a great asset in establishing rapport. They may be close enough in age to adolescents to understand their struggles with the indignities of a hospital, and may therefore be among the young patients' most empathetic listeners.

Students may be assigned the most difficult and complex patients in order to gain experience. In addition to the experience, however, the student needs support. The hospital system can be frustrating to students, particularly when it intrudes on their relationship with the child and family. In some cases students are told when, how, and where to relate to the parents and children, despite the fact that they may have more time available than any other member of the health care team. Student assignments may include one or two patients, whereas staff carry the responsibility for an entire unit.

In spite of her eagerness to be of help, the student nurse often encounters difficulties in working with families. From the family's standpoint, it is disturbing to see a continual wave of new faces in the course of hospitalization; each new nurse will ask essentially the same questions but use her own methods, to which the family and child must adjust. Some families refuse to let a student nurse take care of their child. No amount of inducement can overcome their prejudice against inexperience. In other instances student nurses may be afraid to ask questions about patient history, care, plan, or detailed history and thus be intimidated by the family. Some inconveniences will always arise, and the staff should assess what is best for the patient, the family, and the student in each case.

In the terminal phases of illness, it is extremely difficult for both the family and the patient to relate to a new person—certainly to organize their thoughts to answer questions they have answered countless times before.

This is the fourth student we have had in two weeks. When she asked me how I feel about my child having cancer, I let her have it. It was ridiculous. I felt bad later because I knew they were doing what was required for their history.

The staff can and should support both sides. Procedures take longer when a beginner is in charge, and may be more painful as a result; on the other hand, for lack of confidence many students are more cautious and more gentle than experienced personnel. Some families prefer students and come to their defense when necessary. Several parents were greatly upset by a particular staff physician who had a habit of dismissing the advice of students, emphasizing the fact that they were "just students" or "just residents." What the parents found disconcerting about these reminders was that the staff physician, although experienced and a specialist, would see the child once a day, overlooking the fact that students were there continually.

The care and attention given by some students may be a source of continuing comfort to parents through hospitalizations and the postdeath period. One medical student assigned to a terminally ill child was profoundly shaken by the death. Distraught and unable to talk, she literally ran from the room. "What do you do or say?" she asked a nurse. "I just can't think of anything." Together they returned to the room. The student said, "I'm sorry. I really loved Milroy," then abruptly left the room. Months later, the parents said that this single example of compassion meant more to them than any other.

HOSPITAL AIDES AND ATTENDANTS

In our system, those who give the most direct patient care are the least trained for such responsibilities. Hospital aides and attendants, who may have only 2 to 6 weeks training, sometimes care for ten to twelve patients. They may be high school or nursing students working part-time or the long-term health care personnel who are the backbone of the unit.

Because they lack a degree, their ability to provide expert care is often overlooked. As a result of their care and the time they spend with the child, many families become very close to them. In the demanding course of terminal illness no facet of patient care is menial.

When I was in high school working as an aide, the head nurse said I'd be an excellent nurse, so she gave me all the cancer patients. I didn't realize it was because the RNs didn't want to care for them. I blundered a lot. I'd see nurses sitting at the nurses' station and they would make remarks about how I loved it and then laugh. I did love my work. I found the most beautiful patients. The RNs were the ones missing out. Now 10 years later, as a nurse I care for terminally ill patients and love nursing.

Aides do the heaviest physical work on the unit, for which they receive the least pay, support, and attention. They clean up after the staff and stand in the background literally and figuratively, but they also may have more intimate knowledge of the patient than anyone else.

FAMILY PHYSICIANS

When a terminal illness is first discovered by the family physician, a question that frequently lingers is whether the symptoms could have been detected sooner. She or he wonders whether something was overlooked, and whether the disease could have been prevented.

Some family physicians refer the child to another facility after diagnosis, and thereafter the only contact they have with child and family is through the specialist in charge. Some physicians continue to follow the child through his or her illness and even become involved in certain aspects. One of the most important functions of the family physician is to provide ongoing support, particularly if the family is a long distance from the referral center.

Sometimes the relationship between the family and family physician deteriorates quickly after the diagnosis. Some parents blame the physician for not detecting the illness sooner or for giving them misinformation. For instance, one physician who was not aware of new technology in a subspecialty told a family that their child would not survive the first hospitalization. If they wanted to do any sightseeing, he said, they should do it en route to the hospital. He did not know that new therapy would allow the child to live for years.

EMERGENCY HEALTH PERSONNEL

In recent years an emphasis has been placed on specialized training for emergency health care personnel, and their expertise has paid off in saved lives. They, too, become involved in the crisis facing the child and his family. They are the start of the lifeline in the emergency setting. Many families report that they received telephone calls or letters from emergency health personnel inquiring about the child's condition. Others received sympathy cards after the obituary had appeared in the newspaper.

MEDICAL TECHNOLOGISTS

Medical technologists may not have extensive personal contact with the child, but they do become well acquainted with his history through lab slips and blood results. Often the technologist is the first to know the results of bone marrow tests, spinal taps, blood work, and other laboratory tests.

Since they realize how critically ill the child is, and know about remissions, relapses, and ominous symptoms, it is not uncommon for medical technologists to be concerned and upset. In fact, a frequent complaint of theirs is that so few people realize how much they do care. "All they know is that we stick them, sometimes lose the tube, or have to repeat tests that show abnormal results," one said.

As with other members of the staff, the children have their favorite technicians. The relationships may be short in duration, but they can be strong while they last.

THERAPISTS

Respiratory Therapists

With modern technology, respiratory therapy has become a specialized area in the treatment of the critically ill. It is used for the newborn with respiratory distress syndrome (RSD), in postoperative care, and for children who have been coded. Frequently the respiratory therapist means only painful procedures to a sick child, treatments such as clapping, postural drainage, suctioning, or evaluating whether an endotracheal tube should be reinserted or discontinued.

Because the therapist is so often involved with the most critically ill patients, she or he frequently confronts death and emergency measures.

> Few people see us as anything other than intubators, clappers or croupette providers. When I see those kids get worse, I think, My God! That kid may never see another day. I wish I could be the lifeline for every one of them. You ache but you have to go on to the next patient.

Physical and Occupational Therapists

These two types of therapy are often combined. New technology and the emphasis on total patient care have made the use of therapy more common in the treatment of the dying child, severe burn patients, amputees, and children with birth defects, injuries, or deformities secondary to their disease.

Physical and occupational therapists frequently offer hope for rehabilitation. It is a tremendous achievement to enable a child to resume some of his normal activities, and as a result, these therapists become involved in the child's and the family's life. Understandably, a therapist may be upset when a physician recommends no therapy because the child is terminal. "Doesn't he know that the terminal child is living now and needs everything he can get to make his life easier?" he responds in protest.

Play Therapists

Play therapists are often deeply moved by the child's death since they have had the privilege of knowing the child in an entirely different way than other members of the health care team. They see the fun side, the human aspects of the child, rather than the clinical ones.

> I feel I'm giving something special to these kids. Then I realize what they're giving me. I'm overwhelmed. Their illness and death are a real personal loss. I not only have fun with them, I get to know them. I love them. I see them grow as well as die.

The play therapist provides not only fun but education, developmental milestones, and opportunities for social contacts; most important, he or she provides hope.

A play therapist may give the family a chance to be away, and offer the child a reprieve from the unpleasant aspects of hospitalization. Sometimes the child is allowed to go on passes with the play therapist to games, movies, picnics, and so on; thus the semblance of normalcy in an otherwise abnormal life is preserved.

RADIOLOGISTS

Diagnostic radiology, nuclear medicine, and radiation therapy are the radiographic aspects of caring for the child who is terminally ill. The child becomes accustomed to the waiting room, learns which technicians are sensitive to the discomfort of a hard table or a peculiar position, which are best at injecting the nuclear material for diagnostic procedures, or who gives a surprise candy or lollypop after therapy. Radiology technicians are aware of the seriousness of the illness when they observe metastases, primary tumors, severe cerebral dysfunction, multiple fractures, etc.

> I viewed those films and I knew what was ahead for that child and his family, or, better yet, what wasn't ahead of him. Each month when he has his routine chest (bone scan), I pray they're clear of metastases. I begin to dread them as I know he does.

A technician may see a child change in the course of an illness from a vibrant 3-year-old to a quiet, debilitated 6-year-old with no sparkle. Often, experienced technicians claim they can diagnose a child by looking at "the outside," without seeing the x-rays. A picture on the view box can tell them that a child has little or no life left ahead, only the indignities of chronic illness or irreversible injuries.

PHARMACISTS

Both community and hospital pharmacists become well acquainted with the child, from his first course of conventional therapy through remissions, exacerbations, and experimental therapy. They see him go from Tylenol to codeine to Demerol to morphine and finally to no prescription at all. "I know the diagnosis by the prescriptions I fill. I also know how he's doing. I know when things are getting bad. My heart aches."

The pharmacist has opportunities to become acquainted with both parents and child. A personal relationship may grow out of conversations with the child in which he or she enumerates the medications taken, how they tasted, whether they helped, what side effects they produced, and so on. Some children will tell the pharmacist what should or shouldn't be given to other patients.

Pharmacists may be distressed by the side effects the child will have to face as a result of chemotherapy, even though the therapy may lead to a complete or partial remission. "In the long run, it will be more comfortable, but temporarily it will be hell." It is especially difficult for the pharmacist to deal with young parents of children he knows from experience will die. Realizing how desperately they hope that this drug will be the one to make their child better or live longer, the pharmacist is drawn into their personal world of grief.

THE OTHERS

In addition to the special groups discussed in this chapter, there are other individuals whose lives are sometimes, perhaps accidentally, touched by the family and the child who is dying. A social worker who sets out to research the financial support available to the family may find himself assuming a role in helping the family cope not just financially, but also emotionally.

Business office and medical records personnel may develop sympathy for the dying child and his parents whom they know only through telephone conversations or fleeting contact at the time of admissions or dismissals.

One secretary who interviewed admitting patients showed so much care and concern that returning families requested that she help them. When children came to the clinic they would visit her. "I guess they know I love them," she said. "I feel I'm part of their care, yet most people around here think I just shuffle papers."

Business office personnel often have painful moments despite their distance from the life and death realities of the hospital. As one secretary noted, the business office is one of the stops parents must make after their child has died.

"We come face to face. 'My child died, what do I do now?' they say. I stand there and cry with them."

Telephone operators whose function is to pass on information, deal with emergencies, or try to reach physicians after hours are often remembered for their courtesy and their competence. Housekeeping personnel may add a touch of personal support. Volunteers, engineers, a campus patrolman who saves a parking space for the family, motel and hotel owners who offer special considerations to the family, taxi drivers, or bus drivers are all people whose lives repeatedly touch those of the family and the child who is dying.

Part Three

Illness and Death

Chapter 7

The Beginning

It's just something you read about but it doesn't happen to you.

Why did this happen to us after all we have had happen to us?

I don't want to be here. This isn't our life.

WAITING FOR THE DIAGNOSIS

Diagnosis marks the juncture of two radically different lifestyles: the one before diagnosis, which was normal, and the one after, in which the future is unknown and at the mercy of the child's illness. No single event, with the exception of the child's death itself, has a greater impact on the lives of a family. The parallels between diagnosis and death are frequently alluded to: both are periods of excruciating stresses ending with the realization of a parent's greatest fear. For some, however, the diagnosis itself is the end.

> You feel you can't win. You've lost everything anyway. You're afraid of what else you'll lose or what will be taken away next. It is a horrible, indescribable

feeling of loss, numbness, and disbelief that now your world is coming to an end. That's all you think about. Everything has ended! All the hope that is presented for treatment and palliation means nothing. There is actually no hope — only death.

It seems impossible to the healthy in our society that children with all their resiliency can be ill to the point of death, and that nothing can be done about it. Parents accept the usual childhood illnesses with equanimity — some are even relieved when the child gets them while young, as if this satisfies the requirements early and leaves the rest of the child's life unimpaired by ill health.

The nagging symptoms (e.g., bruising, fevers, weakness, headaches) may cause no great concern at first, but this changes abruptly when a parent sits in front of the family doctor, whose demeanor is solemn in contrast to his or her usual cheer. Never before had he seemed this concerned about anything. "This needs to be checked out by a specialist. It could be something complicated. I'm covering all angles, you understand." From now on the unknown will always be present in some form or other, and this in itself is terrifying.

Everyone appears to be greatly concerned about the child. If the child is in the hospital, a discussion may ensue about transferring him to another facility pending the outcome of consultations; or it may be asked whether the child's condition is stable enough to permit a transfer. The support the family receives from friends and relatives at this time has an undertone of fear.

In the meantime, tests and more tests follow. Endless questions go unanswered, and those which the family finds too frightening or too threatening to verbalize are worried about in silence.

In a matter of hours the family may be faced with the diagnosis, or it may be days or more before they learn anything. Leukemia, for instance, can be diagnosed in a few hours once an adequate bone marrow specimen has been obtained, stained, and read. In the case of other illnesses, the child may have to go through endless testing, biopsies, or even major surgery before a diagnosis is reached; even then there may be uncertainty. Even when the diagnosis can be arrived at quickly, the parents agonize until the results are in. They should be prepared by the physician for what is taking place. As one physician says to parents during the preliminary period:

I'll worry with you. I know this is a terrible time, but I have to be honest. I don't feel it is honest or kind not to tell you that the results could be a serious disease. I just couldn't walk in and tell you out of the blue. I think you already have the feeling that we are all concerned about your Jimmy. We surely hope that all this will turn out as we want. Until all the results are back, I could only give you haphazard answers or assumptions. I will explain what I know as we go along and as soon as we have anything, I will tell you. If we have to order other tests, you will be told the reason.

TRANSFERRING THE CHILD

The process of transfer to a large medical center may postpone the diagnosis. Transfers can take several days when the situation is not considered a medical emergency or if the child's condition is not sufficiently stable to allow him to be moved.

Many families who are referred to a medical center complex come from small communities. For them, leaving a familiar setting for a huge, chaotic city is terrifying even without the burden of a very ill child. Some families admitted that when they were told their child would be transferred to a large university medical center, their first thoughts were not about the child but of the logistics—the fear of dealing with city traffic, where they would stay, how they would get to and from the hospital.

Just getting to the medical center may be a problem for some. Because the child is quite sick, they worry that something may occur en route that they will be unable to handle. Unless the family is familiar with the city and the medical center, they may encounter many obstacles in approaching the hospital: parking may be difficult, the center may be sprawling, ill-marked, busy, and depressing. The stories related by parents about the problems they had before they found the right floor in the right wing of the hospital would sound comically improbable if they were not so commonplace. By the time the family reaches the unit, they may be exhausted, bewildered, and hungry, and have little patience with anyone or anything that threatens to cause further misery.

AFTER ADMISSION

Once the child is admitted, another delay stands in the way of the final diagnosis: one more round of tests. A number of tests performed before the child's admission have to be repeated, the purpose of which is to establish baseline data at the new institution. In some cases, slides, x-rays, or other data are not sent with the patient; in others, the quality may be so poor that an accurate diagnosis cannot be made. Frequently the tests have been altered for various reasons, or the lapse of time between the original tests and the time of admission requires that they be repeated. The repetitions and delays may seem unnecessary to the family and the child, but with straightforward explanations, most families will understand. It may also be a comfort to the family to know that what is a major undertaking in a small community hospital, even starting an IV, for example, is a minor task to the staff of a large hospital who routinely test and care for children.

Television melodramas have influenced the expectations of many people who enter hospitals. They expect their experience to be similar to what takes place on a television show in which, regardless of the rarity of the disease, it can be diagnosed, treated, and neatly wrapped up at the end of the hour. Some families use these shows as a standard to judge the care and treatment they receive. They assume that television dramas are based on some smoothly functioning hospital that runs more efficiently than the institution in which they find themselves. The primary ingredient that is missing from the television script is the anxiety of families after admission. This is what characterizes the real-life experience.

As one would expect, waiting around for a diagnosis intensifies anxiety, allowing the family time to reflect on the incongruity of the situation.

> We've always been such a healthy family and our children are so well. My parents, grandparents, and even great-grandparents are still living.

Parents are at the mercy of experts. They must play the waiting game like others before them. If they rush the results, some error in diagnosis may be made or the wrong therapy may begin. Also, they fear the staff's reaction if they become too persistent.

Thrown into a setting they abhor, fearing the diagnosis of a possibly incurable disease, they meet other parents whose children have been pronounced terminally ill. The incoming parents become vaguely aware of what problems, grief, and stresses the other families are facing.

> These children look so bad and yet their parents are functioning and talking about what is wrong with their child with what appears to be calmness and acceptance. This is not a hospital, it's a horror house.

> Once we got to the unit and we saw all that was there, we literally hid in Donnie's room. We just couldn't stand to see what was outside. We haven't seen cattle that sick and I don't think cattle have been treated like that. They took children into the treatment room and you could hear them cry. You would see people all over the place — children with casts, tubes, poles, on carts, in wheelchairs with dressings, and, worse, without dressings over horrible wounds.

A whole spectrum of grief is before their eyes. But terrifying as it is, the family cannot run from it because their child is a part of it. Even hiding in a room is disturbed by thoughts that one must leave at some point. When their child goes for tests, x-rays, and the like, they are torn between wanting to go along and offer support and the fear that, once there, they cannot even support themselves let alone the child.

The lucky ones find out it was all a mistake, not what the doctors suspected. After being put through the experience and having tentatively prepared themselves for the "worst," they return to the safety of their homes, but not without some profound changes in their outlook.

WHEN THE NEWS IS BAD

Parents who have waited for varying lengths of time before the final diagnosis is made are finally led off to meet with the specialists.

> Why did they have us come down here when the other parents talked to the doctors upstairs? Does this mean it is so bad? Maybe not—he wants to apologize for putting Frankie through all those tests, and he is embarrassed about it.

> He kept saying, I'll tell you everything, but when we asked this morning, he said we would have to wait until later. Well, it is later!

In some instances the room is crowded with interns, residents, nurses, and students, with hardly enough room for the main participants—physicians and family. Some parents want relatives and friends to be included, or, in a few select instances, older siblings. The number of people at the initial meeting depends upon the openness and the philosophy of the staff and family.

The physician may lead up to the diagnosis in a variety of ways. He may give the diagnosis immediately or may precede it with an explanation of test results and of what the results mean to the child. Diagnosis of fatal illness is nothing less than excruciating for both the family and the professional. The latter must tell the family that he can offer neither a total cure nor hope for long-term survival. Moreover, he cannot cure, perhaps not even treat or prevent, the complications of fatal illness. The child may have years to live, and in that time perhaps something will be discovered to change the incurable to curable. But not today.

For most parents, the greatest fear at this time is of losing their composure in front of all the people gathered in the room. Even when there are few people present, parents are afraid of breaking down completely, wishing to be out of sight before this happens.

> They had given us a cup of coffee, but I knew I would spill it if I tried to drink it. I'd also probably throw up. I couldn't light a cigarette I was shaking so hard. I wanted to yell, Shit! shit! You're lying!

Parents may be afraid to ask questions even though they are given the opportunity. Sometimes, this is because they fear they will sound stupid. Other parents refrain from opening their mouths for fear of losing control. An overriding concern is being judged sufficiently intelligent and stable to merit the staff's confidence.

Some parents may be too numb to ask questions. Even at a much later date they have no clear recollection of what transpired.

> After I heard the word "cancer," I couldn't tell you what else he said. I heard things like statistics and treatment and some words that sounded awful for the treatment, but for repeating it all or knowing what he said, I couldn't. I

just wanted him to shut up and let us get out of there. I was burning up and ready to explode. I thought the conference would never end. But at the same time I didn't want it to end because then we'd have to face Jenny.

Other parents are surprised to learn that they asked intelligent questions, but most can recall little of what took place during the first conferences following the diagnosis.

After the conference some parents want to be alone. Most do not want to see their child immediately, yet they do not want to be far from him. They fear losing control, particularly the first time they see him. They also want to protect the child from all that lies ahead, and may ask what to tell him.

The need for privacy, for time to sort out what they have been told and what they have to look forward to, may compel them to leave the hospital—to go outside, or, if they live in the community, to go home. Home is usually the wrong place, however, because of all the reminders of the child.

Early on, most, if not all, parents picture their child dead or suffering intractable pain. This thought is so overwhelming, however, that few parents express it. Their fear is that normal people would think them crazy or horribly perverted. They are greatly relieved to learn that other parents shared similar, frightening thoughts. After the initial shock subsides the picture of death comes less often.

WHAT TO TELL THE CHILD

The rapport the staff has with the child, the child's condition and age, and the family's and staff's attitude toward openness are all factors that determine what and how much the child is told about his or her illness. Parents of young children are quite often fearful of facing them and their questions. They may contemplate withholding the diagnosis, until they are told how unrealistic such a course would be.

Some parents request private time with the child behind closed doors. Others want the staff to accompany them and give support as well as explanation. It is always advisable to have parents present when the child is told, so that everyone knows what is said.

Some parents who return from seeing the child tell jokes and make light of the situation, while explaining through tears that somehow they will all make it.

THE OPEN SETTING

The extent to which parents can participate in the child's care will depend on the institution. Therapy, if any, must begin if there is any hope of survival. Within a brief period after the regimen begins, the child begins to undergo changes, which may include alopecia, pain, nausea, vomiting, cushingoid effects, amputation, or other surgical disfigurements. In open settings, parents are not only informed about what is taking place, but frequently asked if they understand the care and treatment.

In a closed setting, the only news that filters down to the family is news that will not "upset them." While such an atmosphere protects the staff, it does nothing for the family's tranquility. They fantasize either the best or the worst in order to feel in control of a situation that is essentially incontrollable. They may withdraw from the situation completely, fantasize about a magic cure, or convince themselves that a mistake was made.

The staff's own attitudes determine whether family and child feel they are accessible. The pattern of communication between the staff and parents is established at an early stage. In some cases parents are discouraged by certain staff members from approaching them with their questions because of the curt treatment they receive. In other cases they are told what to ask and what not to ask.

> My parents don't have problems. I tell them what their problems are and I tell them the solutions. They don't have to come any more for advice because I have told them everything they need to know and what they can anticipate. If they have sex, another child, or take vacations, everything will be all right. Since I can tell them ahead of time that everything will be taken care of, they don't have to come to me all the time for advice.

Under such rigid restrictions no parent would think of approaching the staff. Obviously the door has been closed.

Parents evaluate staff members on the basis of how much they know and how receptive they are to questions. Staff members who are able to explain disease processes or impart medical knowledge are equipping parents to participate in the child's care. The all-too-familiar health care setting that mandates that everything be done through, to, and for the patient is one that excludes the family and patient. The family's dignity and right to carry out functions of care should always be respected. In general the health care team should evaluate when it is appropriate to include the family, and make the care of the child family-centered.

CONTINUING TO HOPE

Until death is pronounced there will be hope. But the quality of hope changes throughout the course of the illness. After the initial hope that a mistake was made comes the hope that the situation is not *that* serious, that there will be a long-term remission, or that medical science will discover a miracle cure in the interim. Finally, the hope is for death with dignity and without pain, and, after death, that loved ones will be able to cope with the grief process without being completely devastated.

Chapter 8

The Reprieve

Every month I think this could be the *month. I act like I'm not concerned, but I'm really scared. Our science class skipped the section on cancer. I know why the teacher did it. There is always this tension with everybody who knows my diagnosis. When I'm in remission the staff tells me I'm no different from anyone else. They ought to live my life and realize that's impossible.*

WAITING FOR REMISSION

After questions about the amount of pain, and the time and manner of the child's death, parents most frequently ask about the possibility of remission. If the child goes into remission, what are his or her chances for it lasting or for a possible cure? How long will the induction period take, and when will the remission come? There are, of course, no definitive answers to any of these questions.

The parent's anxiety is increased when the child's induction period is excessively long—although to parents and children this period always seems endless. When the induction period is stormy, or the child has been critically ill, parents fear that the remission will never come. The assurances of the staff are dismissed as only words to make them feel better. They begin to think of the promise of remission as a diversion to relieve their distress and not as a medical reality.

Some children have special problems during remission, making it impossible for them to escape the threat of disease, even temporarily. There is even less reprieve for those who need repeated admissions due to toxicity, routine therapy, or side effects of therapy. Technically a child in this situation may be in remission, but he still faces the problems of disease: his bone marrow cancer may be in remission but the chemotherapy he needs produces gastrointestinal ulcers, making it difficult, sometimes impossible, to eat, talk, or sleep.

When the parents and child are told that remission has been attained, the child expresses immediate relief. This is true even of very young children who sense the good news by the reactions of others. The parents too, experience relief, yet for many it is not joy, but merely the knowledge that the first great obstacle has been overcome.

The child is rarely in remission at the time he is released from the hospital. Usually there is another waiting period before remission actually arrives. When it finally does come, it allows the child and the parents to begin a new life. Life will never be altogether normal again for them, but the family can be together again, at least for an undetermined length of time.

Both parents and child may have ambivalent feelings about leaving the hospital. Although the hospital seemed at times like a prison, it afforded protection when the diagnosis was made. At home they have no button at their fingertips to bring help from the nurses; there is no one to answer questions, take over when they are afraid or fatigued, or to give support when needed. And yet the first trips back to the clinic, the hospital, or the doctor's office cause them to relive the traumatic process.

MAKING THE ADJUSTMENT

At the beginning of a long-term remission the family will tell themselves that they are blessed because the child is not in the terminal phase. Time is in their favor, they say. The course of remission is characterized by denial of the illness, bargaining, and vascillation between accepting the reality of diagnosis and hoping that a mistake was made. With its reprieve, the remission brings strong fears about the return of the disease. There are days when parents can honestly say, "I forgot about it. I didn't think about the diagnosis or death." But there are also days when parents think of nothing else.

To an outsider, everything looks normal. The child is out of the hospital, living at home, perhaps even back in school; the parents have gone back to work. It is difficult for outsiders to imagine that the disease is still ravaging the child when he or she looks so good. Few people outside the circle of close friends and relatives know what the child and the family are going through during the "good time" of remission, hoping as they do that the bad times are over. The family more than anyone wishes this were true.

Many parents are afraid to risk living normally again. They feel that normalcy is a pretense, an impossibility, or else too risky owing to the child's unstable condition. Regardless of how well the child does, they know the prognosis is still the same. They cannot relax when things are going well because they are constantly trying to prepare for the time when remission ends. Despite their caution, however, parents still have moments when they are utterly convinced the diagnosis was an error.

The word "normal" has a mocking sound for the parents of a terminally ill child. How could anybody possibly be normal when they have a fatal disease? What normal means in this case is that the child can be treated as he was before diagnosis—his place in the family is restored, his responsibilities resume, discipline returns, and his optimism is encouraged. Treating the child normally gives him a reason to hope.

Remission is often characterized by uneasy silence, pseudo-happiness, and an artificial lifestyle meant to suggest normalcy. Many parents live in fear that mentioning the disease will bring it back. They hope the reverse is true, that is, by suppressing their thoughts about the disease it, too, can be suppressed.

As the visible side effects of disease and therapy decrease, a heavy burden is lifted, and the family can draw a sigh of relief. However, some parents feel they should worry for the child because he seems unconcerned—as if worrying might forestall or avert the inevitable. "If heartburn, ulcers, tears, and diarrhea will do it, then he's cured."

Usually, the child's reactions and moods are mirrored by those of his parents. Remission is real when the child acts normally and feels normal in spite of a required medical regimen. As the child returns to a preillness level of activity, it is somewhat easier for the parents to put the harsh facts of diagnosis out of mind.

THE CONTINUED NEED FOR SUPPORT

In some cases the family receives more support after the child goes into remission than before. For other families the reverse is true: the assumption is that they don't need as much.

When the threat of impending death appears to have vanished, the family may suddenly seem approachable again. The child's illness seems less frightening, and even the fear of contagion, which kept some friends at a distance, is no longer present.

Many families who are accepted by friends in the remission period report that they are ostracized once again when they resume talking about the disease and their fears and depression. At various times in the course of illness, especially at times of crisis, support from friends may resume. But in periods when they think the family should be enjoying the respite, some friends do not want to see them depressed.

MEDICAL CARE

Throughout remission children must return for many kinds of therapy, medications, physical examinations, and so on. When the child is young, he or she cares only about getting through the various procedures and is relieved when they are over. Older children dread both the procedures and the results they may bring. Results will determine whether the child remains in remission and on the road to a possible cure, or whether the day of relapse is coming.

The parents and child watch intently all persons who are concerned with the child's care. Every smile, frown, quizzical look, or facial expression can inspire terror or relief.

I only think of negative things, isn't that terrible? I keep a happy face, but each time they frown or stammer for words I know the next thing they will say will be bad.

Any change in procedure or routine, with or without an explanation, causes alarm. With a change in protocol or a test "to be on the safe side," their anxieties soar until either the new procedure does become routine or the results prove negative. "I never feel positive that things are okay. I guess I'm just pessimistic."

Clinic visits are an exhausting experience for the parents and child. Fear of the procedures, the procedures themselves, the trip to the clinic, the wait, all drain them both physically and emotionally. Now that they are experts in the system, parents and children alike know by many small signs—facial expressions, the time of a telephone call, the tone of the speaker on the other end—what the results are before being told. Parents confess they find themselves thinking the worst despite their outward calm. They may try to allay their fears by saying, "I know everything is fine. These bruises are normal for his age." Only after the results are available are the fears verbalized.

I was sure that he was out of remission. I couldn't sleep the last several nights trying to prepare how to tell him that it was back and he had to return to the hospital.

They are constantly prey to the notion that "if I say it out loud, it will happen."

Some visits I feel better than others, but there's no time that I am totally comfortable and feel secure with no doubts. There are times that I would be more surprised if he came out of remission, but I feel I always have to be prepared. I begin to relax for a short while until a few days before the next visit. People just don't realize the fears are always with you. Little do they know. I guess it's out of sight, out of mind. I wish I could live that way. Some can or, at least, they say they do.

When the parents suspect the child is going out of remission, routine visits become intolerable. The trip to the hospital will be all too short, while the wait for results may seem interminable. Their lives become an exercise in waiting, watching, wondering, and worrying. "I look at her, and I know that something, somewhere, is ravaging inside her, just waiting to come back."

The family and the child need assurances that they are responding appropriately, both physically and emotionally, to their ordeal. They also need to be assured that fellow patients are doing well. Knowing that other families experience the same concerns and relief is uplifting to parents and child. The course of other children's illnesses influences their state of mind. It can either give them hope for a long-term remission or dread that something terrible is ahead.

PROTECTING THE CHILD IN REMISSION

During remission it is difficult for parents not to go overboard in their attempts to protect the child from a return of disease symptoms. In part their behavior is motivated by guilt over the initial diagnosis. Many parents keep daily logs of the child's condition, which makes them feel they are approaching the child's care scientifically. Without this record, parents are never quite sure whether a physical manifestation is innocuous or a signal of relapse. The mother of a leukemic child confessed that she pulled her child's lower eyelids down to check his hemoglobin so often that the child "is going to have bags bigger than mine. I didn't pick up the disease in the beginning. I feel I shouldn't miss it the next time."

Every ache, pain, symptom, or remark is scrutinized. In some cases, however, children conceal or deny complaints, fearing they will have to be readmitted or that a painful procedure will be performed.

In spite of the parents' solicitude, they often debate whether to call the physician with their child's complaints or wait until the next scheduled visit. If they call and the complaint is easily resolved over the telephone ("No, that kind of behavior would not be at all unusual."), their fears are temporarily allayed. But there is always the chance that the doctor will not be so reassuring.

Some parents are not satisfied by the doctor's (nurse's) reassurances over the telephone. They want the child to be seen. If, however, the staff decide the child should be seen, the parents may feel the child is actually relapsing and they have cheated themselves out of a few more days or weeks at home.

Eventually most parents begin to live from one bone marrow test, x-ray, clinic visit, or therapy session to another as the remission goes on. In between, life is more normal than at any time in the course of the illness.

I began to realize that no matter how much I worried, I couldn't prevent the return. So I decided to begin living again. I probably won't have that long a time. I'm beginning to relax more than I ever have; I think Monty is, too. It's been long enough so that I no longer remember some of the awful things.

With longer remissions there is less tension, because parents eventually realize how little they can change by worrying. Moreover, there is constant outside pressure on parents and child to forget their fears. They are bombarded with reassurances: "The disease is gone, what are you worried about? Everything's going well. It's been taken care of—he's probably cured." At times, such confidence on the part of others is infuriating. "No one realizes what it's like to live with this unknown known. You have to shut up or you're shut out. That loneliness adds to the pain."

While some people are telling the family to relax, others are doing just the opposite. Friends and relatives may observe how ill the child looks, or how meager his appetite is, or comment on all the ill effects of therapy. With every mark of pain there may be someone to remonstrate with the parents, "How could you?" Faced with this kind of pressure, parents invariably feel more guilty. Their resolve to treat the child "normally" is met with strong resistance from their critics.

LONG-TERM REMISSIONS

Long-term remission is a new phenomenon resulting from breakthroughs in medical technology. The longer the period of remission, the closer it will come to the maximum length of time in which the disease may be contained. Then relapse becomes imminent, and some families feel they have not taken advantage of the added time.

> I thought I would feel more relaxed at the end of so many months or years. When Gordy was diagnosed, I thought this length of time was a miracle— something unattainable. Now I'm terrified. I know he will relapse any time. I felt that all along but I feel it more now. Nobody can go on forever, can they?

Some long-term remissions are thought to be the miracle the family prayed for. If the remission goes beyond the maximum time predicted, the family feels it is living on borrowed time. Seldom will families share such feelings with others, however, not wishing to appear ungrateful for the extended time.

Some children reach the point of being taken off medication or therapy. (Parents at times even take their child off therapy without the advice of the health care providers.) Instead of bringing relief, however, stopping treatments may create fears that the disease is free to return once again. A reduction in the number of required visits also precipitates fears that any new problems will not be caught in time. The family prayed and planned for this moment, but it does not bring comfort and calm they expected. Instead of "Why me?," they now ask, "Why not me?"

The child can now be like all other children. No therapy, no frequent visits to the clinic, no side effects to make her stand out from her peers. The child is delighted, her parents relieved at her relief, yet they have mixed feelings about being on their own. Time becomes the chief opponent.

END OF REMISSION

As the disease continues its course, the remissions come less often and are shorter in duration. Each one is an attempt to deny the disease and its consequences that does not succeed. Time becomes more precious. Parents relive earlier remissions and bargain for just one more. But they become steadily more rare, and finally stop completely. Yet the inevitable that all have tried to prepare for is somehow always unexpected when it does come.

Chapter 9

The Ultimate Reality

I broke up and became more hysterical this time [the first relapse] than I did at the time of diagnosis. I was too numbed and scared. I didn't know anything of what was ahead. Now I know and I'm frightened.

Most families agree that the first relapse is the worst. The return of disease not only confirms the accuracy of the diagnosis, but also sweeps away the dream of long-term remission and the hope for cure.

It frequently happens, especially during the first remission, that parents think a relapse has occurred, but are told after extensive examinations that it was just a false alarm. When a relapse does come, they continue to cling to the hope that it is another false alarm and not the real thing. Other parents are bolstered by the hope that things might change for the better even after the child has relapsed. Still others do not consider the child terminally ill, despite the relapse.

LEARNING OF RELAPSE

"I have known since last month that this would be the month," one parent said. Some parents are told in the clinic that there are signs of a possible relapse, but that they must wait for the results of tests. To hear the results at a clinic makes some parents and children feel cheated because they have had no preparation. Others are grateful for prompt confirmation, especially if they anticipated the relapse.

> Let's get it over with. I can't stand the suspense any longer. My stomach is in continual knots prior to each clinic visit, even though outwardly I tell everyone that it will not return.

Some parents do not want to be told at clinic. They are afraid to cry in front of the child and staff. They want to soothe the child, but the atmosphere seems inappropriate. Yet if they are told when the child is not present, they must still face him.

Families who have been told over a period of months or even years that the child is unique in his response to the illness usually are harder hit by the news of relapse because they have not been prepared. Similarly, when the first remission is short, the parents and child have an especially difficult adjustment to make, not only because they have been denied the chance to resume normal living but also because they may have been denying the very existence of the disease. "Did we do something to cause the short remission? Was there an error in treatment?" they ask.

STARTING OVER

There is, of course, no opportune time for relapse, yet there are times when its occurrence is particularly hard to endure. Relapse always seems to come when special events are planned by the family, or on birthdays, the eve of a holiday, or when the child appears to be settling back into a "normal" life. "If it had just been a month later he wouldn't be missing school," the parents say. Or, "Couldn't it have come after the semester (or the play, the prom, the football season, our vacation)?"

The readmission to the hospital brings with it the painful memories of the first admission as well as a host of new anxieties and disruptions in the family's life. Regardless of the number of relapses, the transition from life at home to life in the hospital is never orderly. Arrangements for the return to the hospital and for care of the other children as well as explanations to relatives and friends must be handled at a time when the family is trying to cope with the change and make the emotional adjustment.

Parents should be allowed to participate in the care of their child when feasible and desired. Continuity of care is vital for the child and family. The weeks, months, or years of freedom and relief from active disease suddenly end, and the dependence of parents and child on each other suddenly becomes stronger.

Both parents and child may have forgotten what procedures, regimes, and routines were involved in hospitalization. After readmission, they all seem to take longer, and to be more painful. Remission seems as remote as if it never took place. "We are back where we were years ago. We haven't made any progress, and I know there is even less hope now."

It is important that any decisions that have to be made at this time are made with the help of the family. The available medical technology, the individual circumstances of the family, and the child's physical and emotional condition are all factors that should be taken into account in the decision-making process.

THE RETURN OF ANGER AND FEAR

The anxiety and dread that have been suppressed during remission return when the child is readmitted. With exacerbation of the illness, the good days are forgotten, and parents think only of the dismal future ahead. They are angry. "It is not worth all we have gone through," they say, thinking of the long trips to the hospital, the child's pain, and the many, often agonizing, periods of waiting.

The parents' anger can be vented in many ways: at the staff for not listening or for predicting the return of the disease, at all the tests that are useless, but nevertheless cause more pain, at themselves for not accepting the possibility of relapse, even at the child himself.

In many cases, parents feel themselves responsible for the illness, but they are also quick to blame the staff for its alleged failings. Many parents feel they were lied to about the duration of remissions. Some deny that they were told the disease could return. They may charge that the staff lied to them because the relapse was earlier than predicted. The parents of one child who had metastases to the lungs denied having been told that this was even a possibility. "We were never told it would spread," they said. Earlier, however, they had expressed relief when the child's x-rays had been clear.

Families of children who relapse shortly after the discontinuation of therapy feel this was a causal factor in the relapse. Special problems or mixups also cause anger. After her child had received an overdose of therapy, one mother began to time the treatments, measure and check medications, and require all personnel to wear name tags carrying their titles.

With the return of the disease, parents and child are once again beset with fears, primarily of pain, death, and their inability to cope. They have seen others in similar situations, and they begin to understand how imminent these developments are for them.

The disease will once again manifest itself by its outward signs, e.g., seizures, bruising, bleeding, masses, paralysis, pain, or blindness. There may also be additional complications or new manifestations for which parents and child are unprepared.

Parents fear that the staff will make mistakes, or that mistakes already made have not been discovered. Procedures generally become more frequent and painful, last longer, and are more difficult to perform. A relapse is frightening even if the child does well, because the changes he or she experiences are so radical. They may include weight gain or loss, anorexia, alopecia, mouth ulcers, nausea, vomiting, as well as emotional changes, causing acute distress to child and parents.

LOSING CONTROL OVER THE DISEASE

The search for answers, meanings, or causes that took place at the time of diagnosis now begin all over again. Relapse brings more pain, heartache, and expense, more hospitalization, with less available therapy or chance for cure.

The disease's predictability is infuriating. At times parents think it would be easier to have an atypical than a typical case, as they understand the terms, because then they would not worry so much. At other times, they despair of not knowing what lies ahead so they could prepare for it. "If the road ahead could be mapped out, I could be better prepared for even the bad times. Then I could cope better." There is no such thing as "perfectly normal" or "routine" with any disease. The unpredictable, the unexpected, enters their lives. To some parents this seems worse than a disease with a predictable course that can be statistically calculated. What they really want to know is Why? Why the relapse at this time? Why the short remissions? Why the inability to get back into remission?

As remissions become shorter, and relapses more frequent, the fear of unexpected death or unforeseen problems such as hemorrhage, seizures, uncontrolled pain, or respiratory distress, becomes stronger. Parents are afraid that frequent relapses will prolong the agony, comparing their child to other children who have gone before him. They know time is becoming short and therefore more precious, yet they wonder if the suffering will ever end.

Chapter 10

The Terminal State

I wanted to know what to expect for myself and my child. I have never been to a funeral, let alone a child's. I wanted to know how they did it, why they did it, how they coped. I could see myself and my child in that funeral home. It was so painful, but I felt I grew from it, and even though I thought I wouldn't make it, it gave me strength. I also realized I had some time and they don't.

It just hasn't hit me yet. I guess it will pretty soon, but I feel so different than I thought I would. I'm calmer. I don't feel hysterical. I feel a sense of peace. I'm glad it's over. No more waiting, wondering, worrying, fearing. No more pain for him. Now we can start living.

The terminal state can be divided into three stages: the terminal phase, which may last weeks or months, in which relapses are frequent, remissions difficult, and complications multifold; the terminal period, when the inevitability of death is recognized and affirmed; and the terminal event, which includes the hours preceding death itself.

The reactions of parents, relatives, child, and staff are very individual during these stages. But both child and parents try to look beyond the present to face the inevitable death.

In the final stages of illness, time is both a friend and an enemy. It passes too fast during pleasurable moments, but drags interminably when the child is suffering or in pain. This may be especially true just before death for the family who wants respite from its own suffering.

In an extended terminal period, the parents (and the child) go through "highs" when the child's condition appears improved. The parents' responses reflect the child's moods. "When he rallies I do. I fall when he does," said one mother. Emotions oscillate on any given day. A parent may become euphoric over the slightest transitory change, for example, an increase in blood gases, an improvement in the child's color, decrease of pain, easier respiration, a slight smile, or a decrease in bleeding.

BARGAINING REOCCURS

Despite all the prepatory grief and the defense mechanisms that have been used, the terminal phase marks a renewal of the process of bargaining. During the child's terminal course, bargaining goes from extravagant demands to humble requests: experimental procedures, double doses of therapy, or new therapy may offer hope for one last remission. Finally the request is for enough medication to relieve the pain, for a coherent conversation, or a painless sleep.

Bargaining may be construed as a sign of weakness when other parents use it, yet is not recognized as such by the parents themselves. Some parents report to staff members that another family is unable to face the inevitability of their child's death. Meanwhile they themselves are assiduously bargaining for the life of their own child.

Even though bargaining may be frustrating to the spouse, relatives, or staff, it is an important aspect of human grief. When the family says, "We're sure he's going to die, *but* possibly he'll respond for a short time," the temporizing effects are apparent. It is a way of gradually reducing hope. When the child does not respond to treatment, the alternatives change. "We're sure the child is dying, but let it be quick, without any more suffering."

When hope is clearly disproportionate to the patient's condition, parents need help in facing the inevitability of death. A staff member may ask parents how they think the child is doing. If parents respond with excuses and defenses, the staff member may then comment on their obvious uncertainty. Frequently this produces tears and an admission that they know the child is dying.

THE RETURN OF ANGER AND FEAR

Everyone involved with the dying child is angry at this stage; their emotions range from moodiness to blind rage. Great restraint must be exercised by the staff not to snap at parents or give excuses when they are accused of failure to communicate, a lack of concern, or not providing adequate care. The anger and depression are normal — the child's death is not "fair."

As the illness progresses, events and experiences that first seemed shocking and unbelievable become part of the parents' and child's lives. Families describe the hospital, with its routines, examinations, and lab results, as their way of life. Eventually, they may become critical about everything in the hospital: The care is bad, the lights go unanswered, the food is unappetizing, medications are late, procedures are not performed, or are excessive, or too painful. Sometimes these accusations are not just projections, but reality. "What is the point?" a father may ask himself during procedures, when he knows the child has only death ahead.

Parents may become angry if others talking about the future of their child when it is so obvious that the child has none.

> He knew he was dying. It was just three days before he died. They didn't allow me to talk about his death. They felt so uncomfortable with it I knew I'd better be quiet. Maybe if I didn't try to talk about his dying they wouldn't have concentrated on the future. I found that doctors and ministers can't talk about death. They can't handle death. Everybody ran away the more his life ran out.

Many parents feel wronged by the staff but they are afraid that if they express their feelings the staff may retaliate by neglecting the child's care or refusing to keep the parents informed of what is going on. After the death, the parents may vent their anger. One family slammed the door to the child's room after he died. "Keep out! You've bungled enough."

Some parents are hypersensitive to the contrast between their own feelings and those of the rest of the world. Other people seem to be oblivious to the impending death of their child. Inside the child's room there is an air of appropriate solemnity, but outside nothing seems to have changed. It seems irreverent to the family that anyone who knows that the child is dying can try to live a normal life. A get-well card saying, "Hop out of that bed and bounce home," or a bumper sticker stating that "happiness is a family night at home" seem to typify the rest of the world's stupidity and indifference.

The Fears Are Unchanged

"I can't tell now what his cries mean and that scares me. It's as if I don't know my own child." The fears of child and parents in the final stages are essentially the same ones they have had all along: pain, the type of death, the impact it will have, the reactions of parents and child. In discussing the situation or their own feelings about impending death, parents often cue the staff: "We've seen other children who have a great deal of pain. I don't think I can stand that. Will they let us know when there is nothing else they can do? Will they let him suffer?"

You get up in the morning for another day of waiting for his death. You dream nightmares and wake up in the morning, if you sleep at all, and find that your fears start in again. It is never-ending. You fear not being able to help, let alone cope.

Any change in the child's condition, appearance, sensorium, therapy, or emotional status brings fear that death may be imminent. When parents are afraid, everything about the disease seems beyond their capacity to understand.

Often the parents want the child sedated even when this is not medically advisable. In such cases, the parents' fear of the pain the child is experiencing has become exaggerated. Their assumptions are based on the composite of what they have seen, and what they have heard about other parents' experiences. Fearing the worst, they want the child and themselves protected.

ABANDONMENT

Abandonment becomes a problem in the terminal phase. When this phase is lengthy, the family may reach the point of saying, "I can't put up with anymore, especially the pain and uncertainty." The parents' involvement in the care of their child may taper off. The change may be gradual as their other activities increase; more time is spent with other parents and other children, or in counseling and giving emotional support to others. The change may also be sudden. Personal, business, or family matters all at once take them away for longer periods of time. Usually the change is in sharp contrast to their earlier behavior, suggesting abandonment or depression. In some cases, parents are making an attempt to escape the mounting demands of terminal illness and to renew their ability to cope. In others, they want to cling as fast as possible to life to try to prevent the loss. Eventually, they cannot withstand the physical and emotional drain of more ups and downs, more rallies, or more experiments. These feelings bring more guilt—they are not loving parents by society's standards.

> Oh, my God! We have to go through it again. It's not fair. I know people must think I'm an awful mother but I can't stand to see him go through this anymore. I don't think I can stand to see him go through anymore.
> —The parent of a child who died a year and a half later

ACCEPTANCE OF DEATH

At the end of a long-term illness, many parents begin to reach the stage where they can accept the death of their child. The stage is more readily reached when the child is free from pain and appears at peace with himself. The reverse is also true at times: When the pain is great, acceptance, or perhaps resignation, becomes easier.

Parents may realize the inevitability of death and even say that they accept it, but they do not always believe what they say.

True acceptance means realizing that there is no hope for survival—only for a quiet, peaceful, and dignified death. The "best" for the child is not a prolongation of his or her existence but its natural termination. Once acceptance has been achieved, the parents may become impatient for death to occur.

I know she can't live. I know it is inevitable and I'm comfortable now not having to grasp for cure, miracles or new therapies. That makes other people pretty uncomfortable with my attitude, but I have peace now. I'm ready. I just hope it doesn't keep going on and on. We're all exhausted.

The family who accepts the child's death may be censured by relatives, the staff or others who find their attitude incomprehensible. Because those involved are not always at the same stage of grief, the one who reaches the stage of acceptance first needs a great deal of support.

DECISIONS THAT MUST BE MADE

When death is close, the family is confronted with numerous decisions, e.g., whether the child should die at home or in the hospital, whom they want for support and decisions about transplant donations, autopsies, and funeral arrangements. The staff should be sure parents are fully informed of their options, and give them support and help in making the decisions.

Dying at Home

Families who want their child to die at home are not faced with the decision of whether to prolong the child's life, and possibly the pain. Some parents make this decision by themselves, in the beginning. They greatly need the support of staff in carrying out their wishes, as well as assurances that they will be accepted if, at any time, they want to return to the hospital. Generally these families need frequent contact with the health care team.

Many families who want their child to die at home are reluctant to present the idea because they think it may anger the staff. Taking the child home means privacy and freedom from medical routines, but many families are afraid of "what it will look like." They also lose a continual support system.

When children die at home, whether expectedly or unexpectedly, the parents may begin to question their decision. "Would my child have lived longer in the hospital or if we had called the doctor? Should we have given more medication? Observed him more closely? Was he more uncomfortable than he needed to be?"

Transplant Donations

A decision about transplantations must be made soon after the death, if not before. This option is not always feasible because of the cause of death. When a donation is feasible, the option should be discussed before in order to facilitate the procedure, and because some parents are upset by the idea immediately after the death. For some, transplants symbolically continue the child's life.

Autopsies

Parents may be angry or insulted when the suggestion of an autopsy comes up. In some cases, the prejudice against autopsies is so great that the reaction is explosive: "No more mutilation! No more pain! You only want the medical students to practice."

Parents sometimes consent to an autopsy because they feel it will help other patients. They may also feel this last act will contribute to a future cure.

The child himself may request an autopsy. Whether this request is honored should be decided by the personal persuasions of the parents. Regardless of their choice, they need support. When parents are compelled to make a decision against their will, guilt and anger inevitably result. There may be situations when families have no choice about the autopsy—such as when death occurs in questionable circumstances.

Immediate Decisions

Some of the most painful decisions the family must make following the death involve choosing the funeral home, the type of service, the casket, and what the child and family will wear.

> I wasn't sure if I wanted her to wear her favorite dress or save it for us. I felt selfish whatever decisions I made. I couldn't stand to go out and buy something. We decided on her Easter dress. She had only worn it for two hours and she was so proud of it. At the last minute I couldn't stand to bury her Girl Scout pin and badges with her. I had to keep a part of her with us. Do you think I did right?

> I looked at that empty casket and knew it would be his last bed.

APPROACHING THE TERMINAL EVENT

The routines generally continue during the terminal period—hemoglobin watches, respiratory therapy, bathing, etc.—and some parents regard the continuation of these routines as important signs that the staff has not given up. Other parents are irritated that their child has to be disturbed by routines that seem ridiculous and superfluous. Yet, fearing repercussions, they often deny themselves the right to request discontinuance.

Even in an open setting, parents may be reluctant to make certain requests or to discuss certain aspects of the child's death because of a tendency to project their own responses. They seem to be saying, "If I think it is inappropriate, they must think it is inappropriate, too." Because of their emotional state, parents begin to worry about the truth being withheld from them. They are afraid they will do or say something to lose the staff's confidence. They wonder if the staff tries to protect parents by not telling them what lies ahead or how serious the situation is. Are statements like, "I don't know," or "No one can predict," true or are they merely stalling tactics?

There is no way parents can prepare for the uncertainties or the unforeseen developments. The uncertainties make any plans for the future impossible, even though the future may mean only "this afternoon" or "tomorrow morning." Nevertheless, in the final hours before the child's death parents feel the need to organize and prepare. Will a favorite staff member be with them when the child dies? Many parents anguish over the choice of being alone or having others present at the time of death. (They may have no choice.) They wonder whether support will be forced upon them, or whether it will be available if they request it. They may fear that the staff will take over their parental role as primary care givers, or whether the staff will fulfill their roles if they are unable to do it themselves.

DEATH

Hours or even minutes before death the child may rally to a state of surprising alertness. In some cases, parents regard this lucidity as a last treasured gift. In other cases it may be a painful experience, since they know that so little time is left for a last conversation or caress. The child may have just spoken his last words, grasped for a hand, settled into a parent's arms, or expressed his love and gratitude for all his parents have done.

The child's death may also bear no resemblance to the preceding description. In many television dramas and movies, the dying person is well-groomed and goes gracefully. In real life, death may be ugly and shocking. In their anger, families who do not see their child die gracefully may express a desire to bring actors, directors, and producers to stay in a hospital and learn what "the real thing" is like.

Parents are often surprised that the child looks the same after death, apart from a slight color change. Other children may have multiple changes. In the last minutes or hours the child's temperature may drop rapidly so that immediately upon death he or she may be extremely cold to the touch. This may be both repulsive and frightening to the parents. Many do not want to touch the child after he or she becomes cold and rigid. Parents may also be unprepared for the respiratory changes, discharges, etc., that can be frightening.

Some parents scream, while others are too numb to express any emotion. They may or may not feel guilty about their behavior at the time, but in the postdeath period they will relive this moment again and again in torturous detail, or, in some cases, in order to seek consolation.

> Ours at least was loved and well cared for even though she had to suffer before her death. Some children have no chance. Parents don't know what happened to their child if he was kidnapped or murdered, or how he suffered, or if he was alone before his death. Those other parents who beat their children have to be crazy. At least our child knows she was loved and we didn't beat her, hurt her, or leave her.

Chapter 11

Sudden Loss

I felt I had no control, couldn't get ahold of myself and didn't really want to. After all, I wanted to scream to the world that my child might be dead and they won't tell me anything. I felt like I was losing my mind. Maybe that would have been better. Then I wouldn't have felt the horror I did.

Death may be preceded by weeks, months, or even years of preparatory grief in cases of chronic illness, severe anomalies, or irreversible injuries, but when it finally occurs, it still causes shock. In the acute setting—that is, sudden unexpected death—parents not only suffer shock but are often left without support. The extreme grief, the profound sense of guilt, the obsession with finding answers make the death that comes without warning a much more difficult experience.

Accidents are the second most common cause of death among children after the first year of life, and often they occur under the most grotesque circumstances:

I saw them resuscitate a person on "Marcus Welby," but he was an adult. I was afraid I would do the wrong thing and perhaps kill him. Now he is dead and I didn't even try to help him except to scream and yell for help.

And when I saw him laying in the street, he looked so tiny—not the huge 7-year-old I had been yelling at. I had even dared him to go out there once more—"That will be it," I said. Oh, God, that *was* it!

I heard a crash. I was scared that I would wring his fat little neck if I went right away, so I set the timer for 5 minutes but I don't think I waited that long. I don't remember hearing the bell. When I went in, I found him with the bookcase pulled over on his head. If I had just gone immediately, I'm sure that he wouldn't be dead now.

When death results from an accident, the guilt is often compounded by the fact that parents feel at fault because of their carelessness. Even when they are blameless, they feel they could have prevented the accident or death by simply being better parents. They blame themselves for whatever happens to their children, especially when the consequences of their acts are harmful. Using the most spurious and convoluted logic, parents find some tiny infraction, which may have had no direct bearing on the accident, to make themselves culpable. One mother whose automobile was struck by a drunk driver going through a red light blamed the accident on herself because she delayed her car trip to talk to a friend.

Because many parents find themselves unable to act after an accident, as a result of fear or shock, they may look back on the accident later and feel responsible for the child's death.

THE EMERGENCY ROOM

When the family reaches the emergency room of a hospital, the experience they encounter may further traumatize them. Because of the extreme pressure to save the child's life, the parents may have the child snatched from their arms by people who disappear without any explanation.

Many parents, in their numbness and disbelief, seek privacy away from the crowded emergency room. But privacy is usually not to be found. "Being around all those other people in the emergency room made it all worse. There were loud drunks and people crying and yelling. We just weren't up to that."

The following questions are typical of those that parents (or friends and relatives or staff) recall being asked in an emergency setting. Obviously the questions depend on the nature of injury or death; not all of them are applicable in every situation. The reason for such questions may not be clear to the parents, and, in some cases, these questions may be asked quickly by the physician or nurse who is rushing back and forth into the room. Parents worry about the accuracy of their answers, knowing that their answers may affect the outcome. If they cannot recall the answers rapidly, they fear they may look stupid or uncaring. They need reassurance that the staff understands and allows for their hesitancy because of the emergency situation.

What happened? Has your child been sick? Is he normally healthy? How would you describe your child? What is his past history? What was your pregnancy like? Normal delivery? Did he have any problems at birth? When was your last visit to your pediatrician or family doctor? what is his name? How old is your child? Is he normally small or large for his age? What is your age? Does your child have any allergies? When did he last eat? Is he on any medication? Did you give it? Why not? Are his immunizations up to date? Which ones did he have? Did you try to resuscitate him? How did you do it? Have you ever done this before? What was the first thing you did when you found him? How long did you resuscitate? Did you continue during the trip here? Have you lost any other children suddenly? How long was he dead before you found him? What position was he in? Did you move him or wait until help came? Since you weren't there, who is your babysitter? Is she reliable and competent? Where's the sitter now? Were there other children around? Do your frequently leave your children with sitters? Why did you leave your children alone? Is your child baptized? Would you like him to be?

These additional questions have often been asked of parents whose children die suddenly and unexpectedly:

Did you feed him anything new today? Does he vomit easily? Did you hear him? Did he cough or choke? Did you feel something was wrong when you went to check on him? When did you last check on him? How often do you normally check on him? Does he usually take a nap? How long does he sleep? Was there anything unusual when you put him down to bed? Why did you check on him? What position was he in when you found him? Was he covered with a blanket, pillow, toy? Does he normally sleep with these? Was his head caught? Did you immediately check when you heard the crash? What was his color? Was he cold when you found him? Could the other children have been in the room while you were out of the room?

When children have been injured in accidents, many of these questions may leave parents with the impression that the staff finds them negligent, even though this is not intended.

Does she play outside without supervision? Do you normally leave things out where children could reach them? Was she ever a patient here because of an accident? Is the gasoline always near the pilot light? Are heavy books normally on the top shelf? Can she normally open doors? Cabinets? Drawers?

A medical history taken in a crisis often sounds accusatory. The manner in which the questions are asked and a short explanation at the beginning, which can be reiterated during the questioning, can reduce the guilt in the postdeath period, even if time is very limited.

"I know this is hard for you and it is difficult to remember details when everything happened so fast." "Some of these questions may not seem applicable or appropriate for you at this time, so I will explain them later when we are not so rushed." "I know that after I leave you may remember some more details. Please tell the nurse (medical student) and she will relay the message." Statements such as these are reassuring to the parents because they tell them that the staff are working hard for their child and also that the staff regard the parents as important and are concerned about them, too.

From the moment parents walk into an emergency room or intensive care unit, they may be beseiged with questions, sometimes from several different people simultaneously.

Do you have your insurance card? Does the insurance cover this child? We have to have the child's correct birth date in order to get him a hospital number. Do you at least have the insurance number? Please speak louder. Is that January seventh or eleventh? We want to help your child and the number is extremely important.

When there is a suspicion of abuse, the parents are sometimes informed of this by the question, "Have you met Detective Davis or Sheriff Richards?" This happened to parents of a child who died of SIDS; because of a series of misunderstandings, they became suspects.

It is common for parents to become defensive about answering questions. After all, being asked the same question by four different people sounds like a police interrogation to them. "What the hell does his birth have to do with this? What does a normal delivery have to do with an 8-year-old who's been burned?"

The parents' habit of answering questions with questions often reveals their guilty feelings: "By the question about her last trip to the pediatrician, I bet they mean that it was something I should have picked up." "Why do they ask me my age? Maybe they think I'm incompetent." "I wonder if they think that he would have been saved if I resuscitated better? Why do they ask if I have resuscitated him before?"

KEEPING PARENTS INFORMED

Parents should be periodically given updated information on the condition of their child. They should be told away from the noise and commotion of the emergency room, when possible, in some location which is relatively free of onlookers. The more privacy, the better, of course. In a large hospital setting there is generally extra staff available, one of whom could explain in a few words to the parents what is going on behind the No Admittance doors. When such efforts are made the family is grateful.

They had a nurse come out of the room every few minutes and tell us what was going on. She seemed really concerned and very warm. She said the doctors were working very hard but that things looked very critical. She didn't seem afraid of us. She answered our questions and when she didn't know the answer, she said she would find out and she did. We were surprised at that. We thought at first it was a way of putting us off.

A detailed medical report is not essential, merely the reassurance that everything medically possible is being done for the child. A short explanation such as, "They have the heart monitor (this may have to be explained) on Joan. They are very concerned about the slow beat of her heart, but they are giving medications for that," or "Because of the seriousness of George's head injuries, the neurosurgeons, the special doctors for people with such injuries, are now with him. They have to evaluate him before decisions can be made and before they can know the extent of his injuries. They will be out to talk to you as soon as it is possible."

Statements regarding the seriousness of the situation need to be made no matter how obvious this information might seem. "Mr. and Mrs. Jones, we are greatly concerned about Sadie. Things look very critical." It should not be taken for granted that the parents know "things look very critical" (some are not familiar with "critical"). They are in shock. Hearing the words "very critical" or "very serious" from a doctor or nurse, helps them sort out fact from fantasy. Moreover, the families greatly appreciate any news they can get from "someone in there."

Detailed medical terminology serves no useful purpose. Most parents do not understand it, and are struggling to comprehend what is happening and what it means to them. Even when the family has some medical knowledge, they cannot always make sense of all the information because of the crisis situation. Very often the use of medical jargon, with no attempt to simplify, suggests that the staff is stalling, trying to run from the family, taking for granted their understanding, or insensitive to their needs. In any case, families are prevented from asking any questions, which may be the intention. "They said all this like I should know. I was afraid they would think I was a stupid mother if I didn't know what they were talking about."

Assimilating all that is going on in the emergency room is a difficult task for parents. Yet when the child's condition worsens, or he is either near death or has died, the parents often know this without anyone telling them.

All the confusion going on in the room ended and we knew that it was bad. They mentioned that Jess would go to intensive care if he made it. Suddenly everyone seemed to disappear. We knew he was probably dead, although we didn't want to admit it to anyone or each other. They really didn't have to say anything, because what they did, how they ran from us, we felt as if we had the plague. They put us off and kept referring us to one of the doctors. The looks they gave us really said it all.

In an acute emergency there is little time to contact relatives who could provide the family with support. Frequently a mother is alone when her child dies. Perhaps all efforts to contact her husband have been unsuccssful for one reason or another. This situation is a delicate one, and calls for a rapid assessment of the following questions: Should the mother be told without the support of her husband, relatives, or friends? Is it possible to get someone to help comfort the mother before the child dies or the mother is told of his death? How long will it take for the father to get to the emergency room or home? Does he have transportation? Is he alone? Who can give the father support? Is he a stable person? How good is the parents' relationship?

When he is finally reached by telephone or has arrived at the hospital, the father's first words spoken out of shock and anger, may be, "What did you do? The baby was fine when I left. How could you let this happen?" He may decide that the staff is incompetent and threaten lawsuits. In the brief time it takes to get to the hospital some fathers manage to get drunk, which may add to their abusive behavior.

Some fathers do not arrive at the emergency room at all, leaving the mother and the staff fearing for their safety. This is why it is so important to evaluate the situation carefully. Under duress, the mother may not be able to answer questions coherently, and in such a case it may be helpful to call on a relative or friend who can give support to both parents while providing the staff with pertinent information.

The staff's conduct is important in maintaining the family's confidence. Remarks made by staff inside a room or in the hall travel on a frequency that only desperate parents can hear. Complaints about not having the right equipment to carry out emergency procedures, or that a physician could not be reached will obviously add to the parents' anxiety. Remarks about the parents' inadequacies are not only unnecessary but also totally insensitive, and display a lack of insight and of professional deportment. Such remarks, if overheard by the parents, can be devastating to them.

INFORMING PARENTS OF THE DEATH

If at all possible, a lone parent should not be told that his or her child has died. As stated in the previous section, if the spouse cannot be present, a close friend or relative should be summoned to provide comfort and support. While the staff awaits the arrival of this person, the parent could be told that the situation is very serious and that the chances for the child's survival are very slim—thus making possible some preparatory grief. By preparing the parent, first by advising that someone be called and second by letting it be known that the child's condition is grave, the staff has conveyed its care and concern.

The explanation given to a family after the death of a child should be short and carefully worded. Many parents have said they wanted to know if their child was living or dead, "but the doctor just kept going on and on and we wanted to know first off how he was." The explanation should include a description of the injuries (or disease process), extent of the injuries, for example, irreversible brain damage, what was done for the child, and probable cause of death.

In deaths resulting from SIDS, parents need to be given assurances that they are in no way to blame. They can be told, for example, "We know of nothing you could have done to cause or prevent this. Your child did not suffer, he did not suffocate. An autopsy will prove what I am telling you."

The information should be pertinent to the situation. Parents want to know, "Did the child suffer? Did she know she was dying? Did she call for her parents? Could we have prevented it? What was the cause of death?"

Parents should have time not only to ask questions, but also to vent their feelings of anger, shock, and grief, and to talk about the child's death. This can help them grasp the painful reality of the death. Parents should also be given privacy—not to be confused with abandonment—to compose themselves for questions and to release feelings that they do not wish to display to the staff. It also helps the family when they see the staff's sadness over the loss of their child.

The way the family is told of the death in some cases constitutes a tragedy in itself. For example, one young couple whose child died of SIDS said they were informed by a doctor who came to the door of the waiting room and said hastily, "He's dead. There's nothing we could do." In another case a young woman was called by the hospital and told that her young brother, who had been driving her car, had been involved in an accident and as a result was "seriously hurt."

> We came into the emergency room. I didn't see anybody around. I told some-one that I was called because my brother had been in an accident, and I wanted to see him. They told me to wait. We stood there in the hall and this nurse came out and said, "He's dead," and handed me one bloody shoe. "That's all we could save." I don't think I said it, but all I could think of say-ing was, "What about saving his life?"

THE LAST VISIT

The decision whether to see their dead child is not always easy for parents; how-ever, the opportunity should always be presented to them. If they refuse, the choice should be honored and respected. They should never be forced. With appropriate support, however, the last visit can be helpful to parents in grasping the reality of the death and beginning to work through the grief process.

Parents need to be prepared in advance for the child's appearance. Because of their shock, the reality of the situation may make no impact on the parents until they actually see their child dead. For this reason, it may be important for them to have the experience, in spite of the trauma it causes. A staff member should be present to give support and to answer questions.

The child should be clean and dressed, and mechanical devices, monitoring equipment, tubes, etc., should be removed. Many families comment that when everything is stripped and removed, the child looked "like a lone corpse on a cart." Leaving the child beneath blankets with no clothing may seem a thoughtless oversight to the child's parents, so staff should see that he or she is clothed.

The visit should be short, but not so short as to leave the impression that parents are being rushed or that the staff has anything to hide. Parents may or may not want to hold their child. The choice is a personal one, and whether it should be suggested will depend on parents' reaction to the visit itself.

Holding the child can be a beneficial measure when parents are working through their grief. It is a chance for a final goodbye, and often makes parents feel accepted as caring, loving people by the staff.

Giving the child's belongings to the parents causes them to feel the painful reality of the child's death. These last items (clothes, bottles, toys) touched by their child are important treasures. Their condition should be appropriately assessed; for example, a bloody, torn shirt might be withheld. Some parents *insist* that every item be given to them. A short explanation, such as "your Timmy's shirt was too soiled," may gently tell the parents it would be too painful or inappropriate for them to have a particular article. This also prevents angry accusations from families who later return, requesting the child's possessions that were "stolen." Insistency, however, should be respected.

I'm glad the nurse told me Zoe's jeans weren't salvageable. I knew just what she meant and I appreciated her caring.

My God, why on earth did they give us Tom's bloody, vomit-stained shirt? They said it was the "rule." Rule for cruelty and insensitivity?

THE PROLONGED EMERGENCY

A crisis that begins in the emergency room often continues for hours, days, or weeks in the intensive care unit. The emotional trauma resulting from the initial accident—the rush to the hospital, the flurry of activity in the emergency ward—is relived when the family see their child for the first time in intensive care.

An intensive care unit is ideal for complex care, but for an outsider it is a terrifying place. The monitoring equipment, the tubes, and the strange machinery, as well as the sounds and odors are new and frightening to the family; all become part of an ordeal that may last for weeks. The lack of privacy and the presence of other acutely ill patients add to the trauma caused by the setting.

Generally, the child is not very alert, but he may also be combative or else totally lifeless. "Does his combativeness mean he is in pain or wants us near?"

the parents ask. "Will all this equipment save his life? Is it necessary?" From the waiting room, the parents see staff members going in and out, yet giving no clues about what is going on except for their grim faces.

> Every code blue they called for the unit, we parents would huddle together wondering who had "gone bad." Is there such a thing as a *badder* bad? We sat there feeling alone, often too scared to talk. Sometimes someone would say something or laugh just to break the tension. We dreaded the footsteps, yet we lived for those reports no matter how sketchy.

The experience that these parents live through is one of extreme torment. Theirs is a vigil that frequently keeps them in a crowded, smoke-filled waiting room, with a television or radio providing background noise. Some parents sit for hours on end afraid to go for food, to the bathroom, or to sleep, in case the child's condition should change and the doctors need to confer with them. When all hope for life is gone, the visits can be unbearable. As long as hope remains, some parents want to stay close by, knowing that every minute with the child may be the last. Others, because of the hopelessness of the child's condition, may visit less, and when they do come they are irritated because the critical stage goes on for so long. Since there is no hope for survival, they want the child's life to end.

THE TRIP HOME

When the final arrangements have been made, and the parents have said the last goodbye to their child, someone should walk the parents to their car, particularly if friends or relatives are not with them. They should be given the telephone number of the emergency room or intensive care unit, and the name of a physician or nurse for questions that may arise later. This reassures the family that the care and concern of the staff will continue.

The journey home from the hospital has been described as "dreadful" by the parents. They may never before have been separated from their child, which makes many feel they are literally abandoning the child.

The parents' emotional condition should be evaluated if they are driving, and in cases where driving is not thought advisable, it would be wise for staff to try to make other arrangements.

Chapter 12

The Postdeath Period

When we went to panel the kitchen, we pulled the stove out and there was one of Mark's Hot Wheels. We both saw it at the same time. We just stood there numb. When I looked up, Jim was white and had tears in his eyes. We held each other and cried. We had only done that twice before—when Mark was diagnosed and when he died.

I thought I grieved before she died. That was nothing. I didn't know what grief was. I did all my thinking at night. Now I can't turn it off. I think I heard her. Sometimes I have gotten up and looked. Her room is empty and then that sick feeling comes over me.

The postdeath period literally begins after the child's last breath, but in this chapter we treat it as the period that begins the night after the funeral. This is the first night of never seeing the child again, but the full impact is not felt at once. Some families describe an intense desire to see their child just once more when returning home after the funeral, even though they know he or she is no longer there. The experience is a prelude to what lies ahead in the stages of acute grief.

From the moment of the child's death, a steady stream of visitors, many of whom had become strangers during the illness, bring their condolences. The family is allowed little privacy in this period, even though they are exhausted from the physical and emotional stresses of the past several days or even years. The telephone calls never stop and so much has to be done that family members may have little time for themselves. They may be somewhat resentful toward all the people who are now willing to help, but were not available before the death.

Anticipatory grief is at an end, and may be followed by a sense of relief that the death is finally over. Many parents are surprised that they have no strong feelings of loss and grief at the time of death, since they expected this period to be the most agonizing. Furthermore, they are often surprised that they did not fall apart or become hysterical. At the same time, they fear that their behavior may be abnormal or indicate that they really do not care. This lack of emotion may bring with it severe depression, pride at having "worked it through," or confusion.

A sense of calm and peace throughout the funeral and the days following is common to many parents. To some, the sight of their dead child may fail to move them in the way they anticipated. They feel only a sense of relief that the child suffers no longer. To others, it is a painful realization that it is all over.

Grief often does not come to many until weeks after the death. When it does strike them, it is often seen as a punishment for having failed to grieve appropriately at the time of death. The parents actually find themselves holding everyone else up at first. They have become accustomed to playing a supportive role during the illness, and continue to do so. When their acute grief begins, they feel a profound sense of failure.

The abrupt change in their lives is staggering. Suddenly there are no more finger "sticks," waiting rooms, clinic visits, blood tests, bone marrow tests, or x-rays. The host of appointments that filled the past weeks, months, or years are gone from their lives. Some families say they would go through it all again to have more time with their child—at least time for one more goodbye.

The demands of chronic illness dictated a lifestyle based on fixed routines and strict schedules; now the parents can return to a normal way of living, but their former lives seem abnormal to them. Time has been marked off by the stages of illness or the onset of injuries: before the diagnosis, after her accident, a month after the infection, the first remission, the second relapse, the change in chemotherapy, and so on. Understandably, some families have no recollection of how life was before the illness. The first adjustment comes with the realization of what life without the child will be like—never being able to hold, see, hear, or touch him or her again.

GETTING BACK TO NORMAL

There is no way to generalize about the time that it takes to get back to normal. A father who is said to be taking the death of his daughter "pretty hard" may nonetheless be back at his desk in the office 3 days after the funeral. A mother who is at least composed in public is assumed to be "doing very well." Often getting back to normal is not so much a matter of the griever's adjustment, but of the adjustment of others to the bereaved.

Parents are often avoided by friends who do not want to hear any more talk about the child or his death. One way people work through grief is by talking about it, but to outsiders this may seem only to prolong the grief. In some instances, friends and acquaintances expect the family to make a swift adjustment to their child's death because of all the preparatory grieving they went through during the long illness.

> I know they have children of their own and I know what they're thinking when they look at me. I don't know what to say and I know they'd rather not talk about the death. They've heard enough about it during the illness. Sometimes I'd really like to talk about it, and then there are other times when I'd rather try to forget, at least for a short time. It helps to feel included. They put up with a lot during the illness.

Some do not understand the family's behavior, and their insensitivity is shown by the comments they make. Parents who lost an adolescent may be told that their adjustment will probably be easier because they have had more time with their child, or that at least he didn't become an addict or a delinquent. The opposite logic is used on parents of a young child: Because the parents had the child for such a short time, they could not get so attached to her. Cliches, a common form of defense, are showered on the family. For dismissing an incomprehensible loss with some erroneous inanity ("The good die young . . ."), an outsider may receive a tongue lashing or be completely ignored.

Some parents must return to work soon after the child's death, while they still feel numb. The thought of returning may be repugnant to them, but the days will be oppressive if there are no preoccupations. Any activity helps fill the hours of pain. "At least at work I can have short periods when I don't think about it."

Getting back to normal means concealing feelings as well as overcoming somatic symptoms: sighing, weakness, fatigue, gastrointestinal upset, insomnia, anorexia, and menstrual disturbances are all very common. Many parents describe days of uncontrollable crying and depression followed by "good" days; the latter turn out to be a false signal that the grief is over. After a period of good days, the parent may be plunged back into the same depths of despair that the parent thought had been surmounted. Depression itself may be such an abnormal feeling that a parent is convinced that he or she is losing his mind.

Nightmares are common during the illness, and even more so after the death. Insomnia that began during the child's illness may now become chronic. Many parents are surprised to find how soundly they sleep immediately after the child's death, only to find several months later during the acute stages of grief that they are suddenly unable to sleep. "Everybody is asleep and I get up and go down into the family room and cry. I spend many nights that way."

When they begin to try and live a more normal life, many parents feel guilty. If they go out to a show, dancing, drinking, or even to a small gathering with friends, they feel qualms of guilt. They fear what others will think, but most of all they question the appropriateness of having fun.

It's just an outward gesture for my wife. I know she needs to get out. My heart isn't in it yet. I laugh and look like I'm having fun and all I can think about is that a month ago we were sitting in the hospital watching Hardy die.

When we went out, I cried all the way to the dance. My husband could have crowned me. I drank because I thought that would help. Then I felt horrible. Then I felt even more guilty—going to a dance and getting drunk. My husband said I wasn't drunk. We can't be hermits, he says.

I get so tired of all the advice to have fun and get in the swing of things. I think if they wouldn't keep harping on it, I would begin to relax.

Obviously there is ambivalence over the new-found relief and freedom. Parents may have had the responsibility for care for an extended length of time, and are happy to resume many of the pleasures they enjoyed before the illness. At the same time, they feel it is wrong to do so.

I don't have to hurry home from the hospital, the store, school, or anything. I don't have to worry whether I am staying too long. I can go to the store, visit friends, attend the kids' school activities, go to church, clean, cook, and not have to hurry and be prepared to leave the oven on for my husband to get an overcooked meal. I can't describe the feeling. I know it took Ellie's death to give me this freedom. But sometimes I feel like screaming and crying. I have to admit that I am enjoying it. I don't have time to grieve.

When the acute stage of grief arrives, their exuberance ends.

STARTING A NEW LIFE

They used to have restrictions, but now the siblings find that the restrictions are lifted. No longer do they have to be quiet or turn friends away. The family can be active, and make plans that were impossible before the death. Yet the family may have grown apart. They are able to be together again, but they feel like a group of strangers. Some families never recapture the closeness that existed before the diagnosis.

The relief that the parents anticipated, and possibly felt at the child's death begins to fade within a few weeks. Nothing they do, no place they go is comfortable.

I feel feelingless. I don't want to have time. I want to stay busy, but I still think. There are times when it seems like a nightmare. It seems horrible. Mornings come and another day to face. Another day of loss.

Many feel compelled to return to the hospital or clinic to visit staff, the floor, and sometimes even the room where the child died. For many parents the visit is painful. They cry as they relive the memories. Some wonder why they bothered to retrace their steps or what the urgency could have been to come to the hospital and go through such a painful experience. Others express satisfaction after the visit, but also feel no need ever to return again. These visits may take place soon after the death or even months or years later.

Some parents continue to return to visit fellow parents and their children, perhaps to show to others that they, too, will survive regardless of the outcome. They also return because they desperately want to talk about the child or to show pictures taken at the funeral home. These pictures are important to many parents whose children suffered from disfiguring diseases. Later in the grief process, the families may find the pictures distasteful and painful, but they help at the time.

RELIVING THE PAST

Families relive the funeral time and again. They want to know what others thought of the service and of the child's appearance, for instance, whether he looked peaceful, or if his suffering showed. The funeral service becomes a treasured memory in cases where it was the kind of service the parents wanted. Parents appreciate the thoughtfulness of people who come to the funeral home or the funeral, and staff members who give readings, deliver eulogies, or act as pallbearers.

In the grief process, the family constantly relives the death and the days preceding it. The child's last words are turned over and over in their minds, his state of awareness and comfort continually assessed. Parents relive the private moments, as well as the waiting period before the death—what the child looked like, his color, his breathing, and his general appearance. All the scars of the child's illness are etched into memory. Some parents are, in fact, angered by the ease with which a cosmetologist removes these marks after death.

Parents recall who was present at the end, what was done to the child, and their reactions. Those who were not there may express guilt about that; those who were alone with the child relive the terror they experienced.

I went to the nurses' station. I told them to check on George, although I knew he was already dead and they couldn't do anything. I just sat there at the nurses' station knowing he was dead. I kept saying to myself, he is dead! he is dead! he is dead! I constantly relive that moment and the fear I had then returns even now. It was like a dream.

Many express the fear that they will never stop thinking about the child; at the same time, they are afraid to stop for fear they will forget him. In some cases, parents who are in the early stages of the grief process find it difficult to remember the child.

I don't want to forget anything. If I do, then I feel as if I will forget him. I can't remember anything other than his illness. If I forget that, I will have forgotten everything about him.

For some time any hospitalization (of themselves, relatives, or friends) brings back memories and feelings associated with the child's illness. Even "happy" visits to the maternity ward are not happy for some. Hospitals become places where death, suffering, and grief originate. "There was nothing but blackness looking down the hall—a kind of oblivion or a state of nothingness."

GRIEF BEHAVIOR

Many parents write their personal story, which turns out to be a type of diary describing their intimate experiences during the illness. The purpose of the account may be to share with others their feelings about what the loss means, or else to publish it as a book. In some cases, the parents feel the account may be useful for research aimed at helping other children with similar problems.

To help them remember, they may play the child's records, look through his scrapbook, writings, or drawings, or set out his picture while writing. Often the inspiration to write coincides with special anniversaries, holidays, or birthdays.

If the child began a project before his death, many parents feel compelled to complete it. Parents will sell or distribute cookies, candy, and so on for school clubs, church organizations, or sports teams to which the child belonged.

Following the death of their child, or even during the illness, some parents become involved in volunteer work for an organization that is concerned with the type of illness or anomaly their child had, for example, the Leukemia Society, the March of Dimes, the Myelomeningocele Association, or the Sudden Infant Death Foundation. The enthusiasm some parents brought to their work during the child's illness may, however, taper off after his death.

Frequently contacts with other parents whose children suffered similar illnesses can be helpful. Some, however, find the associations too painful. "I have to be around normal, happy families," said one father. "I've lived with that for so long that I can empathize, but I think I've had it."

Some parents throw themselves into volunteer work as a way of escaping their own grief. In theory, they work so hard that they have little time to grieve, but actually they merely postpone grief for a time, and eventually they must learn to cope with it.

Volunteer work often becomes a permanent commitment, a type of memorial to the child. In some cases the promise was made prior to the child's death (perhaps even to the child himself) to work for an organization pledged to irradicate the fatal disease. Many parent organizations were founded as a result of this kind of commitment, such as the Candlelighters or the Myelomeningocele Association.

The Child's Possessions

The child's possessions become very precious to the parents: no value is high enough for them. For some parents, only the possessions that the child cared about are meaningful, while for others, anything he came in contact with is difficult to part with. Other parents may want no part of any of his possessions. Possessions are sometimes kept in the room, sometimes packed away in the attic for safe keeping. The items which have special meaning are those that are considered an extension of the child himself: tape-recorded conversations, drawings, writings, even a handprint made of clay. A handprint or fingerprint left on a mirror, or a muddy footprint on the carpeting become treasures to be left untouched. Many parents want to donate the child's possessions to a hospital, school, or other organization—an act analogous to establishing a memorial.

Stripping the child's room may accentuate her absence, so that parents may decide to redecorate or convert the room to some other utilitarian purpose. In cases of sudden death at home, parents may feel they are unable to live comfortably in the house again and move immediately. Some families of children with long-term illnesses move after the death. For others, the house remains a site of treasured memories. Similarly the family automobile may evoke fond memories, and, even though it is undependable, the family cannot part with it.

Resuming the activities the family enjoyed when the child was alive may be difficult after his death. Attending a Little League baseball game, for instance, brings a surge of memories.

> My heart isn't in the things we do now that Mary is gone. I know it isn't fair to the other kids. I just relive so many things. Then I have bitter feelings when I see others not appreciating their kids. Then I think I'm not appreciating my other ones. I can't concentrate.

Returning to the child's school to gather her possessions is so painful for some parents that they make arrangements to have them picked up, or make an early morning or late night trip to the school to avoid seeing other children. An empty locker or desk seems to symbolize the child's departure. Some parents want pictures of the child's desk or locker as if to provide documentation of his existence.

Some parents want to visit school while class is in session to see the emptiness the child's death created. At the same time they want to see what their child would have been doing. Parents may visit the child's teacher and peers to discuss *their* feelings of loss and to hear what the child's death means to others.

The Child's Presence

Most parents describe feeling the presence of their child after the death. Although they cannot see her, literally, they experience the sensation of being near, and can visualize her playing, singing, laughing, or crying. They often describe the feeling as being "so real I think I am losing my mind." Not only do they question their sanity but also the reality of the child's death. "I know I sound nuts, but I know she was there. Sometimes I can see her, but a lot of the time I feel her presence." One mother related the custom she and her child had before going to bed every night. They would give "love knocks" on the wall. Shortly after the child's death, she heard the knock.

> After hearing the knock I sat there reliving his precious custom, thinking I was imagining it. Then I realized his brother was in the room. I thought he did it to make me feel better. He [the adolescent brother] ran into the bedroom and asked me if I knocked on the wall. "No, I thought you did it, or I was just imagining it happened," I said. I knew he wasn't kidding by the look on his face.

Similar incidents are related by other families. One of the most common places to feel the child's presence is at the gravesite. To some parents, however, the gravesite has little meaning, and after the funeral they never return to it at all.

One of the first visits may occur the same day as the funeral. Some parents experience warmth and closeness to the child at the gravesite more than at any other place—at least for a time after his death. Within a period of weeks or months, this special feeling at the gravesite may subside.

When visiting the child's grave, parents generally perform the rituals of kneeling, praying, crying, or observing a period of silence and then talking to or about the child. It is not uncommon, however, for parents who feel close to the child at the gravesite to nevertheless feel awkward about performing such rituals.

The Written Word

The death is irrevocable. There are times when any denial is impossible. Receiving the death certificate is one such moment.

> The day her death certificate came I sat and cried so hard I couldn't read it for 30 minutes. That piece of paper cut the lifeline forever. That was *our* Dedra they typed out so businesslike. I kept rereading the causes. It seemed so impersonal.

Many parents are confused that the cause of death is not the disease itself. Staff can be a great support in explaining complex terms to the family.

It said cardiac arrest, pulmonary edema, and intracranial hemorrhage. It scared us. I thought Glennie died of leukemia. I called the nurse to verify it. I guess you even deny death. That's that last straw you can grasp at.

Income tax time is another painful time. In years past the child was a deduction. There were also deductions for the illness. The year of the death, the illness, the funeral expenses, and the child were deductions. The year following, the emptiness is a crushing void. Parents of adolescents have a painful task when they receive a tax form and must complete the income tax return. "It's like a ghost is over my shoulder," one father confided.

Choosing the grave marker is frequently the last decision the family has to make.

When you see his name and date etched in stone you know it's forever. I guess until then I had it in my mind. I stood there and realized there was no turning back. Now he's only memories.

Spending Money

Spending money, frequently on unnecessary items, is a common occurrence after the child's death. Occasionally buying sprees are the result of doing without in the course of the child's illness or of depression. Families now take vacations, buy toys, redecorate the home, or buy clothes and furniture.

In some cases the parents may be trying to make up to the siblings what they were cheated of during the illness.

I know it won't help, but I just think maybe this will take part of the pain away. How ridiculous. I already know it won't. Afterward, I feel guilty. I think here my child is dead and I am spending money and having a, supposedly, good time. It just doesn't make sense.

Instead of paying medical bills, the family may spend the money on themselves: "They didn't save my child so they can just wait for their money."

Suicide

Many, if not most, parents entertain thoughts of committing suicide. The thoughts may be fleeting, or the parents may have given the matter long consideration and made elaborate plans, even though they are never carried out.

I don't have feelings for anyone or anything. I can't believe they [family or friends] would miss me. I made the child my whole life. I'm glad, I don't regret it.

Some parents begin thinking of suicide while the child is still living, but they have too much guilt to explore the possibility. After the child dies, suicide is more appealing. Depending on the parent's beliefs, death may represent a way of uniting him or her with the child. More often, the motivation is to escape the prison of one's thoughts, to be free of sadness and guilt.

Mothers talk about running their cars into a bridge abutment, or taking an overdose of sleeping pills and forgetting their misery. Fathers often plan more violent ends for themselves. "If I'd suffer, then I would know what my child went through," said one father.

As a result of these fantasies, parents often realize the value of their lives, as well as the potential for inflicting pain on others that suicide has. Parents seldom volunteer information about their suicidal throughts because they seem to be just one more sign that they may be losing their sanity.

Anniversaries

For a time, each day will be an anniversary of the life of the child or of his death. One day may be the anniversary of the diagnosis, another of a remission, a relapse, or a new crisis. The first holidays following death have particular meaning. The child's absence is a reminder that the occasion is not entirely happy. In fact, the majority of families say that it takes 3 years before the holidays begin to be happy occasions again.

Life may go along smoothly until the eve of a holiday, when suddenly the associations with the child's life come to mind, and parents realize how empty the celebration will be.

I suddenly realized I dreaded it so much. I thought I couldn't stand it. I thought I would lose my mind. I couldn't face the holiday or all the relatives. I wanted to scream: "Don't you know what we're going through? Don't you know what we've lost? How can anyone think of happiness?"

In rememberance of the anniversary, some families have memorial services, a mass, or even a special observance in the home. One family had the custom of allowing each member to discuss what he or she liked or disliked about the dead child, lighting a candle, and having the child's favorite flowers. The family agreed that after these discussions they became closer, and more realistic and honest about their feelings.

THE DURATION OF GRIEF

The duration of grief cannot be accurately assessed because each individual reacts in a unique way. Although the stages are similar, factors such as the depth of feeling, former experiences with death, religious philosophy, maturity, cultural practices, and the type of death affect the grieving process.

From observation, it seems that the period of acute grief generally lasts into the third year. At the end of this time many families are prepared to say they feel like themselves again, and are ready to begin living again. Some, of course, make the return sooner, others later.

The first year is one of total numbness and getting used to the idea that she is really dead. The second year you're pretty much abandoned. Everyone *knows* you are over your grief. If you show signs you aren't, then you're in trouble. You feel it is a never-ending process. It isn't like the books you read, or the shows you see. You are becoming totally convinced you are crazy. You feel you can't legitimately blame death now.

Some are quieter about their grief than others, reluctant about revealing the hurt they feel. Many couples do not talk to one another about their feelings until the second or third year after the child's death.

I had no idea my husband felt so badly. I thought he didn't grieve at all. He didn't talk about the child. I thought I was the only one who cared so deeply. I was so angry with him. I finally sat him down and we began to talk. I was so shocked that he had been suffering for so long. I found that I drowned out everyone, thinking that I was the only one who hurt so badly. I had been really selfish.

Siblings may wait as long as 5 years to discuss with their parents what happened. Some talk earlier, or even at the time of the illness, others not at all.

In a very real sense the postdeath period lasts forever, even after a new life is well under way. The new life does not eradicate the loss of the child, who will always be a part of the family.

Part Four

The Nursing Process

Chapter 13

Care of the Dying Child

Staff: *You have only four more taps.*
Nine-year-old: *That only quadruples the pain, you idiot.*

THE STAFF AS EXPERTS

We, the professional staff, are experts to the child and family, whether we feel it or not. We represent a lifeline for the child and his family. If we do not provide expert physical care, they will not entrust their emotional needs and confidences to us. When lights go unanswered, pain medications are delayed, IVs run dry, dressings are not changed, or the host of immediate and necessary health care needs are not adequately met, it is difficult for the child and family to share their fears and anxieties with us.

Realistically, most staff have limited time to spend in "pure" emotional support. But, during the implementation of direct patient care or procedures, the patient can be given a great deal of support through both verbal and nonverbal messages. Touch, attentiveness, respect for the child as a person, explanations, listening—all prove more effectively than words alone that the child is first an individual and second a patient who has a terminal illness. For example, "Timmy,

I know you hate these shots, but I have to do it. I hate to hurt you. You said this vein was the best and to hold it this way was the easiest. I'll help you so we can get done as fast as possible." This explanation conveys to the child that you, the nurse,* recognize his dislike for painful procedures (no shot is painless!). You have told him that it must be done, shown him you like him, and recognized his knowledge of which vein and positioning is best, (children who have chronic illness are usually experienced about such things). He knows that with cooperation it will be done as soon as possible. No false promises or threats are necessary. Children cannot tolerate the anxiety of a long wait or detailed explanations before procedures. Even older children are more tolerant and cooperative when procedures are performed quickly and not drawn out by detailed descriptions or delays. This, however, must be assessed for the individual patient.

PATIENT HISTORY AND ASSESSMENT

Astute observation, patient history, and assessment are the basis for the nursing care plan and the implementation of short- and long-range goals. The patient history, as outlined in Table 1, is applicable to patients with terminal or chronic illness. This history cannot be obtained in one interview. Some of the information may have to be obtained indirectly through observation and assessment. Much of the interview can be conducted with the child and family separately, and the data then combined. It will be interesting to note the differences between parents' and child's answers, for example, in regard to diet, school, relationships with siblings and family members, sexual activity, knowledge and understanding of the diagnosis, etc. Some of the information obtained will change in the course of the illness, so that the nursing history must be constantly updated. The amount of information a child can provide about herself and her illness will depend upon the child's age and maturity and the rapport established between staff and family. The time, manner, and place for the interview must be judged according to the child's age and condition and the family's emotional stability. Solid information can be obtained by one question such as, "Mrs. Smith, can you tell me what a typical day is like?" The interview should be as free of distractions and interruptions as possible. Confidentiality is extremely important. Some of the information obtained may be of such a personal nature that it should not be transferred to the chart. Trust can be permanently destroyed when information is not treated with respect and professional discretion. When a situation arises that is potentially detrimental to the care of the patient, the family and child should be assured that the information will be passed along to the appropriate health care providers. The discontinuance of medication, school phobia, and serious family problems may all affect the care of the child. Supplying the information may not change the situation, but it may provide avenues of support for the child and/or his family during times of great stress.

*The word *nurse* is used to refer to different types of nurses, e.g., staff nurses, clinical specialists, nurse practitioners, and practical and vocational nurses.

Table 1 Outline for Taking Patient and Family History

1 Family history (must be updated throughout the illness)
 a medical
 b psychosocial
 c cultural—language(s) spoken in home
 d educational background
 e consultation aspects
 f other obligations
 g other health care problems
 h nickname or special name child uses (used by others or *only* family?)
 i ages—all members including patient
 j birthday of patient
 k prenatal care, delivery, and postnatal care and history
2 Previous hospitalizations of family members or this child
3 Previous experiences (or knowledge) of persons (other than family) with *same* diagnosis
4 Knowledge *and* understanding of child's condition, diagnosis, and treatment
5 Transfer to referral center (if applicable)
 a by whom
 b for what
 c information given to parents
 d how told—by whom
 e mode of transportation to referral center or community hospital
 f mode of admittance
 (1) routine
 (2) emergency
6 Patient's physical state
 a prior to diagnosis
 b present—length and duration of symptoms, how picked up, by whom
7 Emotional status of all involved—from history and observation
 a previous
 b present
8 Questions asked by family and child during interview
9 Defenses used during interview and at other times
10 Answers and reactions to questions
11 Past health care of child (give age and date)
 a childhood diseases
 b other illnesses
 c trauma
 d surgeries
 e immunizations—needed or up-to-date?
 f medications (including birth control pills past and present—prescriber)
 g mode of introduction of medication
 h other
12 Patient's susceptibility to disease
 a as viewed and interpreted by family and patient (when applicable)
 b as obtained by medical history

13 Allergies—documented or suspected
    a food
    b drugs
    c tape
    d merthiolate or other topical antiseptics or soaps
    e dyes—clothes, food, medication (e.g., IVP)
    f topical anesthetics
    g animals
    h type of reaction, age of onset, duration, type of therapy
    i other
14 Meals and nutritional patterns
    a time of main family meal
    b snacks—when and what eaten
    c breakfast eater?
    d best and favorite meal
    e family routine
    f child's routine
    g types and amount of food (formula when applicable) and fluids
       taken
    h cultural aspects
    i vitamins—if taken, prescribed (iron included?)
    j special diet restrictions
       (1) religious
       (2) cultural
       (3) medical—e.g., diabetes, allergy
    k favorite foods
    l foods disliked
    m family's, others', and patient's mode of coping with k and l
    n recent changes in dietary patterns
15 Sleep and rest patterns
    a nap—times and length (changes on weekends, holidays, summer)
    b bedtime—rituals, time and length (changes on weekends, holidays,
       summer)
    c type of sleeper
       (1) sound
       (2) easily aroused, restless
       (3) poor or light
       (4) recent changes
       (5) changes during hospitalization
       (6) night crawler, wanderer (how handled?)
       (7) nightmares (when and how handled?)
    d sleeping arrangements
       (1) alone
       (2) with siblings
       (3) with parent(s)
       (4) with others
       (5) night light

      e support and comfort for the child (day and night)
         (1) special blanket or pillow
         (2) animal—real or stuffed
         (3) thumb or finger(s) (which finger?)
         (4) pacifier or bottle
         (5) toys—by name (are they available?)
         (6) radio, stereo, earphones, or TV
         (7) other
      f type of bed
         (1) crib—side rails
         (2) single, double, bunk, or youth
         (3) sleeping bag, couch, floor, other
      g type of room
         (1) private
         (2) others in room (who?)
         (3) night light—where?
         (4) room temperature preferred

16 Elimination patterns
      a potty-trained (when applicable) at what age, by whom, how, problems encountered
      b frequency of bowel and urination (number of diapers used)
      c type of stool—color and consistency
         (1) normal—described and verified
         (2) loose—described and frequency (how handled?)
         (3) constipation—described and frequency (how handled?)
         (4) diarrhea—described and frequency (how handled?)
      d pain with urination or stool
         (1) type of pain
         (2) methods of alleviation
         (3) onset, frequency, and duration
      e hematuria or melena—onset, frequency, and duration
      f enuresis and/or encopresis—onset, frequency, duration (how handled?)
      g recent changes—describe

17 Menstrual history (when applicable)
      a menarche
      b flow—amount, regularity, duration
      c dysmenorrhea—modes of alleviation
      d attitudes toward menstruation—patient, family, others
      e type of protection used—pads (kind) and/or tampons
      f sex education—by whom, if understood, comfort with explanations
      g sexual activity (if applicable)—birth control measures (if any)
      h hormones taken or prescribed, including birth control pills

18 Growth and development
      a average ⎫
      b fast   ⎬ as compared to ⎰ charts / siblings / others
      c slow   ⎭
      d family history—turning over, walking, talking, etc.

   e as viewed and described by family, child, and others
   f as verified by medical history
   g as assessed by health care team
19 Prostheses
   a special shoes
   b glasses
   c artificial eyes
   d artificial limbs
   e braces
   f dentures or retainers
20 Special problems
   a hearing
   b speech
   c balance
   d vision
   e paralysis
   f limping
   g retardation or slow learner
   h aphasia
   i other
21 Child's routine
   a home
   b school (include nursery school and preschool programs such as Headstart)
   c social activities—likes and dislikes
   d rest patterns
   e recent changes
   f indoor vs. outdoor child
   g activities and play habits
      (1) quiet
      (2) active
      (3) group-oriented
      (4) loner
      (5) special interests
      (6) recent changes
22 Socialization of child
   a as described by the family and child (when applicable)
   b as observed by the staff
   c preference for socialization with:
      (1) peers
      (2) older children (family or others)
      (3) younger children (family or others)
      (4) siblings
      (5) adults (family or others)
   d ability to get along with others (children and adults)—concerns involved, if any
   e "one-friend" person
   f "many-friend" person
   g no friends

   h slow to warm up
   i friends allowed, encouraged, discouraged — by whom
   j recent moves by the family — child's reaction
   k relationship to babysitter (if applicable)
   l neighborhood constellation
      (1) many children patient's age
      (2) mainly older and/or younger
      (3) no children

23 School situation (when applicable) including preschool (actually goes or plans to go)
   a participation
      (1) of child
      (2) of parents
      (3) attitude toward school and teachers
      (4) amount of absenteeism — verified, causes
   b mode of transportation
      (1) bus
      (2) parent driver
      (3) car pool
      (4) on foot (alone or with friends)
      (5) bicycle, motorcycle, or car (own or family) — rides alone or with friends
      (6) public transportation
   c likes and dislikes
      (1) what child likes, and why
      (2) what child dislikes, and why
   d grades — expectations and reality
   e potential
   f outside activities
   g relationship to teacher(s)

24 Relations with friends and peers
   a contact with by visits, phone, or mail — postdiagnosis
   b parents' tolerance of **a**
      (1) as described by parent
      (2) as observed by staff
   c child's description of friends
   d popular child or loner?
   e any changes anticipated since diagnosis?
   f allowance by staff and hospital regulations

25 Patient's relationship and status in the family
   a to parents — favorite, difficult, or special child — pre- and postdiagnosis
   b siblings — order, number (any deceased — cause)
   c wanted and/or planned for child ⎰ this information may come only
   d unplanned child ⎱ after appropriate rapport has been established

26 Discipline of child
   a as described by family and child
   b as observed by staff

    c modes used—by whom
    d changes during hospitalization and since diagnosis
27 Family constellation
    a two-parent family—if cohesive, stable (by description and observation)
    b one-parent family—reason (unmarried, separation, divorce, or death)—
       is partner known?
    c sibs vs. only child
    d extended family
       (1) supportive—emotionally, physically, and/or financially
       (2) nonsupportive—in what ways?
    e distance from other relatives
       (1) emotional
       (2) physical
    f stepparent(s)—adoptive parent(s)
       (1) participation allowed?
          (a) active
          (b) nonactive
          (c) rejection of—by child, spouse, others, staff, own withdrawal
    g separated and/or divorced parents
       (1) participation or lack as in **f**
    h pets—names, kinds, child's relation to them
28 Family's religion (if any)
    a restrictions of religion (if any)
    b child baptized?
       (1) yes
       (2) no
       (3) to be
       (4) never intended
       (5) not previously intended, but now will or may be
    c child confirmed?
       (1) yes
       (2) no
       (3) to be
       (4) never intended
       (5) not previously intended, but now will or may be
    d church attendance (pre- and postdiagnosis)—regular, occasional, none
    e relationship with minister
    f activities at church
    g signs of guilt—bargaining
    h frustrations of religious teachings vs. emotional reactions now
    i last rites?
       (1) yes
       (2) no
       (3) to be
       (4) never intended
       (5) not previously intended, but now will or may be
29 Occupation of parent(s)

    a inside home
    b outside home
    c need to travel
    d stable employment
    e transient employment
    f seasonal employment
    g employer helpful or otherwise?
    h sick leave, vacation, or insurance compensation
    i regularity of hours—rotation of shifts
30 Financial status
    a impending bills
    b any insurance (group or individual)
    c past-due bills
    d past medical expenses
    e dependents
    f resources available
        (1) bank account and savings
        (2) loans
        (3) family
        (4) friends
        (5) community
        (6) Crippled Childrens' Commission or other organizations
        (7) Medicaid
        (8) other
31 Available transportation
    a car condition (reliable or unreliable)
    b 1- or 2-car family? more than 2?
    c backup help
    d distance from health care facility
    e public transportation—mode
        (1) will be used regularly
        (2) as a backup
        (3) reliable
        (4) readily available
32 Communication (degree and quality) between
    a husband and wife
    b parents and children
    c parents and sick child
    d sibs and sick child
    e parents and sibs
    f parents and other relatives
    g child and other relatives
    h sibs and other relatives
    i parents and school (if applicable)
    j staff and school
    k parents and employers
    l parents and staff

m child and staff
n staff and family (other than parents and child)
o staff and staff
33 Telephone communication
   a one phone (extensions)—location(s) in home
   b no phone
   c party line
   d heavy usage by adolescent sibs
   e used for business as well as family
   f best time to call
34 Probability of marital problems
   a prediagnosis
   b postdiagnosis
   c assessed by family, staff, others
35 Visiting patterns of family—assessed through course of illness
36 Care of siblings
   a during hospitalizations
   b during clinic visits
   c at other times
   d by whom—relatives, friends, consistency
   e where
   f frequency of visits to patient
      (1) allowed—by whom?
      (2) discouraged—by whom?
37 Family's reaction to illness
   a as described by family
   b as assessed and observed by staff
   c sibs' reaction according to family and staff
   d child's reaction according to family and staff
   e grief process of all—stages, defenses, coping patterns
38 Family's previous experiences of loss
   a of parents
   b of other children (relatives, peers)
   c of other relatives
   d of others
   e methods of handling grief

ORIENTING PARENT AND CHILD TO ADMISSION

Table 2 outlines an approach to orienting the family and child after the admission. (The child's age and condition may not warrant his or her participation.) The orientation can be done by the admitting nurse or by a member of the staff. The hospital, which is in a way a home to the staff, is a foreign environment to the families and children. It is easy to forget the terror and shock families are experiencing, particularly with the first admission. The complicated equipment, many strange faces, alien language, etc., are all new to both patient and family. The patient and family can be thought of as guests, and it is the responsibility of the professional staff (which is usually nursing) to lessen the trauma of their adjustment. The adjustment is never easy, but perhaps it can be made more tolerable and less frightening.

Table 2   Period of Initial Admission—Outline for Parent and Child Orientation

1 Provide physical care—if good physical care comes first, then emotional support will follow. Take care of immediate needs:
   a life-threatening situations
   b admittance to unit for child and parent
   c help with initial history and physical exam
   d procedures that are or may be done immediately (when applicable)
     (1) blood drawing
     (2) intravenous therapy
     (3) sedation (when applicable)
     (4) transfusions
     (5) intubation
     (6) restraints (when necessary or applicable)
     (7) measuring height, weight, and temperature
     (8) medications—routes of administration
     (9) bone marrow aspiration
    (10) preoperative preparation
    (11) taps—lumbar, epidural, subdural
    (12) x-rays
    (13) physical exam, possibly several
    (14) special procedures
       (a) pneumoencephalogram
       (b) scans
       (c) tubes: chest
              catheters, e.g., urinary, suprapubic
              CVP
              arterial lines
              nasogastric
       (d) IVP, arteriogram
       (e) tracheostomy
    (15) control of pain and effects of pain
    (16) special equipment required for procedures or monitoring
    (17) pre- and postoperative teaching care
2 Keep child and parent informed and prepared for what to expect—providing liaison
3 Introduce ICU (when applicable) or other unit
4 Arrange lodging facilities or rooming-in for parent(s), as well as meals and laundry
5 Introduce the staff

      a medical
      b nursing
      c allied health care team
      d students
  6 Answer questions
  7 Provide paper and pencil for questions
  8 Write down information—this reinforces teaching
  9 Allow participation of family in care, if feasible
10 Encourage discussion
11 Work out visiting privileges—of family, friends, sibs
12 Explain hectic activity in the unit during specific times
      a crises
      b day shift—rounds
      c evening and night—decreased staffing
13 Explain inability of staff members to stay with parents and/or child
14 Find out about previous experience of family and child with such situations ("Have you ever known anyone, family or other, who has been here before with similar or different problems?")
      a good experience, successful outcome?
      b bad or frightening experience—death?

Nursing staff carry the greatest load of direct patient care. There may be little contact between the physician and the patient and family or between physician and staff in some settings. The total care remains, however, a team effort. No one discipline can do it all. The physical needs of the patient are great, although they vary with the diagnosis, condition, and therapy required. Priorities must be carefully evaluated. It intensifies the family's guilt, for example, if they feel the staff are spending too much time with them, and thus depriving their loved one of life-saving care or needed therapy. When the family can deal with one member of the team as a liaison and resource person during stressful times, they are willing to share their thoughts and fears with that person and can question without feeling they are taking time away from their child. The shock and anxiety that follow the diagnosis make it hard for the family and patient to recall all the facts given to them. A nurse liaison can explain the situation again in lay terminology and provide time for questions and the release of feelings. However, it may take time and numerous meetings to build up a good relationship.

    The liaison person can also provide information while the family waits during resuscitative measures, surgery, or other procedures. The family can be prepared for how the child will look, what staff will be working with the child, the equipment involved, and so on. Families waiting outside intensive care units, surgery units, emergency rooms, or other waiting areas see only who and what goes in and out of the room, and do not know what is going on. In the case of a multiple-care unit, they are not even sure if all the rush of activity is for their child. A question such as, "Do you think Jimmie will get to go home tonight?" may seem inappropriate and naive coming from the parents of a child who has severe head injuries as a result of an accident.

NURSES AS TEACHERS

Teaching is one of the nurse's most important roles. Teaching of the family and child is usually informal. The open setting allows family and child to feel free to ask questions. The diagnosis should be reiterated and explained, and parents should be told about therapy and possible side effects. Preoperative and postoperative teaching, allowing for the parents' (or family's) participation in the care of the child, and reassuring the family are all part of the total care. This places responsibility on the nurse to be adequately informed in all these areas, since misinformation can be harmful.

Explanations of the equipment, therapy, and side effects can be given at the time care is administered. The family can thus be taught the practical aspects of caring for the child. Teaching has more meaning and will be absorbed more completely after the initial crisis of admission and news of the diagnosis. Teaching will continue throughout the course of the illness. Preparation for care is often different from the care itself; for example, preparing parents for the care of epistaxis by showing them how to hold the child's nose.

When a situation arises for which the parents and child have been prepared ahead of time, they are more ready to handle it, and the teaching is reinforced. Communication may have to be made by telephone after dismissal—the family should be allowed to call and, while carrying out their care, receive reinforcement of instructions given at an earlier date. Demonstrations are helpful. The family and child observe the nursing care given and are then better able to proceed correctly. Orientation and education procedures are outlined in Table 3.

Table 3   Outline for the Orientation and Education of Parents and Child

A   Orientation and education after admission and crisis
    1   physical set-up of the unit—tour when applicable and feasible
    2   routines
        a   rounds—teaching and grand
        b   equipment
        c   procedures—explanation of
            (1)   finger sticks—f.s. (or venipunctures)
            (2)   vital signs—v.s.
            (3)   bone marrow—b.m.
            (4)   intake and output—mode of collection
            (5)   temperature taking—mode (centigrade vs. Fahrenheit)

      (6) urine collection—routine and special procedures
      (7) special procedures (which may become routine depending upon the diagnosis)
         (a) spinal taps
         (b) other taps
         (c) venipunctures
      (8) radiology—routine x-rays, nuclear medicine, radiotherapy, scans—tour when applicable and feasible
      (9) medications—modes of administering, required and/or preferred route
    (10) other

3 tubes—IV, urinary, chest, etc.
4 other equipment
5 nap times or quiet times (depending upon the unit, age and condition of patient)
6 bedtime (depending upon the unit, age and condition of patient)
7 entertainment items
  a TV—rental (rules for use), or from home
  b radio, recorder, stereo—rules for use
  c games and toys
8 other entertainment items
  a on unit
  b allowed from home
9 hospital policies
  a on family staying
  b participation of family
  c visiting rules
  d passes
  e learning unit
  f age of visitors
  g for pets—live and stuffed
10 toys from home (welcome when feasible)
11 hospital school participation
  a set up
  b when applicable
  c when available
  d when recommended
  e problems involved
12 introduction of staff
  a explain size of staff
  b different roles
  c different cultures
  d uniforms
  e requirements
  f approximate times for routines, rounds, visits, etc.
  g consulting staff or nonroutine staff

B Ongoing assessments and teaching
  1 child's concepts, experiences, and fantasies of illness and death
  2 necessity for openness
    a for parent
    b for child
    c for family
    d for staff
  3 understanding denial and the grief process
    a child
    b family
    c staff
    d others
  4 overprotection—the constant fight
    a consistency of discipline—by whom administered
    b manipulation—measures used by children and family
    c pressures from others
  5 referrals and consultations
    a during hospital stay
    b after dismissal
  6 introduction of sick child to children with same or similar diagnosis and children with unrelated diagnosis—roommates when applicable
  7 preparation for body (image) changes
    a physical (when appropriate)
      (1) hair loss
      (2) weight gain
      (3) weight loss
      (4) incisions—scars
      (5) amputations
      (6) petechiae—bruising
      (7) prostheses
      (8) striae
      (9) dressings
      (10) other
  8 isolation
    a physical
    b emotional
    c by family, staff, others
    d required by diagnosis (protective, reverse)
  9 behavioral changes to anticipate during hospitalization and after dismissal
    a of spouse
    b of child
    c of siblings
    d of relatives
    e of friends, neighbors, community
    f of others
  10 pre- and postoperative teaching

11 preparation for dismissal
   a clinic visits
      (1) previsits and introduction of child and family before dismissal
      (2) introduction of outpatient staff
      (3) physical set-up
      (4) routine, including procedures
      (5) parking facilities
      (6) length of visit and waiting
      (7) who can come with child and family
      (8) what to bring, e.g., records kept by family, toys, etc.

C Care of child
  1 dressings
  2 tubes—catheters
  3 nutritional needs
  4 medications (including names)
    a none (presently)
    b route of administration
    c time of administration
    d practice before dismissal
    e supply for refill
    f side effects
    g approaches to problems, if any
  5 elimination
    a any problems
    b special needs
    c necessity for measurement (if applicable)
    d observation of changes
    e regularity
    f diet relationship
  6 sleeping pattern
    a observation (within reason)
    b need for rest
    c discourage sleeping with parents or siblings
    d regular time for bedtime and napping
  7 discipline
    a necessity for
    b aspects outlined in **B4(a, b**, and **c)**
    c support of family to implement discipline
    d practice before dismissal
  8 special precautions
    a thrombocytopenia
      (1) modes of stopping bleeding
      (2) restriction of activities
      (3) modes of care until treatment is available
    b leukopenia

      (1) observe for infection
      (2) mode of care until treatment is available
      (3) restrictions
   c equipment—brought from hospital or to be obtained
   d therapy
   e disabilities secondary to diagnosis
   f other
9 return to normal life as far as possible
10 names and numbers of staff to contact when problems or questions arise
11 preparation for return home
   a sick child
   b parents
   c siblings
   d family
   e others
12 family and marital stress resulting from diagnosis
13 referrals (when applicable)
   a community health nurse
   b social services
   c rehabilitation services
   d minister
   e community agencies, e.g., Crippled Children's Commission, Leukemia Society, American Cancer Society, Myelomeningocele Association, March of Dimes, Cystic Fibrosis Association, etc.

Preparing for the first dismissal is frightening to most families and often to the child as well, because the family is now faced with the total responsibility for the child. Follow-up home visits (when feasible), referrals, phone calls, and letters are reassurances of continuity of care and interest.

The scheduled readmission or clinic visit may be only days from the dismissal, but may seem much longer to the family in their new role of health care providers for a terminally ill child. The necessity for follow-up exists for all families. It should not be taken for granted that all families will automatically return when scheduled. This is less frequently a problem in open settings.

At the time of diagnosis, the family needs to be prepared for the onslaught of advice they may face when the child is dismissed and for the many pressures that will fall on them. This reminder is particularly important when preparing families for the period of remission. The family and child must be reassured they can call or return for help when problems arise. Phone numbers should be available to them for 24-hour coverage, and the health care provider should try to establish a comfortable relationship when they do call after the dismissal. Many families are quite hesitant to call, while others call frequently out of anxiety. This anxiety should lessen with reassurance and support.

REMISSION

During the remission period, nurses can help the family and child by reinforcing the idea that a normal life can be resumed. They should also explain the importance of continuing the therapy. It is difficult for some families to understand the importance of continued therapy when their child is "normal," particularly in the case of an adolescent or when the procedures are painful (e.g., bone marrows, spinal taps, venipunctures). We perform a great disservice to the child and family if we produce a period of physical remission but allow the child to become an emotional cripple. The importance of treating the child as normally as possible cannot be overemphasized.

It is difficult, if not impossible, for most parents to discipline the child even when he is in remission. Again, this problem should be confronted at the time of the diagnosis. Parents and patient need to verbalize their fears. Often relatives and friends may also need reinforcement about the importance of discipline. The child should not be allowed special considerations or encouraged in inappropriate behavior. Still, the situation often does get out of hand insofar as disciplining the child is concerned.

The possibility of school phobia needs to be anticipated. This may originate in the mother rather than in the child. It is hard to relinquish, even temporarily, ties that may soon be severed completely by the child's death.

The nursing care plan and history need continual updating in the period(s) of remission. Home visits, phone calls, letters, and referrals are still important follow-ups for child and family. Continuity of care is a necessity. When the child can communicate with empathetic staff members, his attitude will be more cooperative and his trust will increase. This is true of all remissions. The relationships may be established with the first remission and continue throughout the course of the child's illness. Ideally, there should be continuity with both inpatient and outpatient staff. It is encouraging for the staff to see children who have been hospitalized living an active life as outpatients.

Introduction to outpatient routines should be made before dismissals, particularly the first dismissal. (The routines may change when remissions are more infrequent.) The child should be encouraged to meet other children and socialize at home or in the hospital or clinic. The child in remission can provide support and hope to less fortunate children. Sometimes, as the remission progresses, the temporary side effects from the therapy gradually disappear. In other situations, the remission may not be long enough for side effects to disappear, or else the side effects may be permanent.

RELAPSES, EXACERBATIONS, AND COMPLICATIONS

If there has been good rapport during diagnosis and the remission period(s), the family and child will have trusted staff to help them when an exacerbation takes place. Depending upon the condition of the child, the relapse may or may not be a surprise to her, her family, or the staff. Many parents ask a particularly significant staff member to be present when the child returns for procedures such as a bone marrow test, scan, or x-ray, or when the parents or child suspect a relapse. This may be a way of gaining support as well as a bargaining ploy that the presence of a favorite staff member will somehow prevent a relapse.

Both family and child need acceptance regardless of how they respond to confirmation of relapse. The family and child also need constant preparation for such a moment. This does not mean that the relief offered by remission should be constantly marred by threats of relapse. If the child and family have been given support and education, and allowed honest and open dialogue, they will be as prepared as they can be for this traumatic time.

Readmission into the hospital is often quite traumatic. The admission procedures outlined in Tables 1 and 2 may have to be repeated if the remission has been a long one. There may be many changes in staff. While nursing and medical staff will probably have little turnover, house staff and students may all be unfamiliar to the family and child. Moreover, as the relapses grow more frequent, the problems increase. The procedures have to be done more frequently and are often more difficult and painful and yield fewer benefits than in previous relapses. For example, a packed bone marrow may require bone biopsies; adhesions present more difficulty with lumbar punctures; scarring and multiple venipunctures through the months and years mean that multiple injections are required before a successful IV can be put in place, only to infiltrate more readily. The child of any age and the family need a great deal of support to endure these painful and often, to them, useless procedures. Families often turn to the nurse for guidance, support, and reassurance.

CARE DURING THE TERMINAL COURSE

The family needs to be prepared for the possibility of sudden death. They should know that death may occur at any time and at any place (home, hospital, en route to either, during procedures). The preparation is not intended to frighten the family but to make them better able to cope with such an occurrence. How much to tell the family must be assessed on an individual basis; sudden death is more of a likelihood for some patients than for others because of the unpredictability of their condition. Families who are not prepared for this possibility suffer intense guilt and anger when it does happen. There is, of course, no way to predict the exact moment of death in any situation.

The child should be allowed throughout to talk about the illness and impending death. Usually by this time the child has chosen someone in particular to talk to. That person may be a parent, minister, friend, relative, or nurse. It is a person whom she trusts and who will accept her and all her varied emotions. "I knew you wouldn't laugh when I told you I was scared." "I've wanted to talk to you for a long time but I wanted to wait until I thought I could really talk."

"I've got to talk to someone. I knew you'd listen." Such remarks are often openers that children may use. It is important that the child, parents, and family talk with one another. Many unresolved conflicts may be worked out during this time between family members. Confidentiality on the part of the staff is imperative. Questions should be answered openly and honestly. This does not mean brutal frankness: "You're going to die and that's that." Rather it implies supportiveness and honesty, which will protect the dignity of child and family.

Families are often afraid to broach the subject of discontinuing therapy with the physician, for fear of the repercussions. The nurse is often the person to whom they turn after making the decision. Even when the decision is "firmly" made, conveying it to the medical staff is often difficult. It is the responsibility of the nursing staff to pass on such information to the medical staff. Sometimes the decision only leads to guilt after death, and therefore it should be carefully assessed at the time. Most families feel great relief when such decisions are taken out of their hands. They are then convinced that the decision was based on valid medical judgment and not on their own fatigue and heartache.

Guilt intensifies in the terminal course. If the family is religious, its members often experience guilt at their lack of faith, or anger at God for allowing the child to come to this. They feel they should display superhuman stamina—not eating, sleeping, or caring for their needs.

Parents may become embarrassed over the child's and their own behavior if it does not fit their preconceived ideas. They experience guilt over the pain the child is having, as well as their inability to alleviate it. This leads to anger at the staff, who are also unable to do anything.

Past and present conflicts between parents and child, or parents and staff may cause guilt. Parents wonder whether the treatment was adequate, or else, if it was excessive, prolonging the child's existence rather than his life. They become angry and guilty over not being able to speak up to the staff when the need arises. Perhaps the greatest source of guilt is not wanting to be with the child when he dies. Most parents fear their immediate reactions at the time of the child's death. Many have preconceived ideas of how they will behave and are afraid their behavior may be inappropriate. Most fear they will completely lose control, thus losing face with the staff. The older child experiences much of the same guilt as the parent. Allowing family members to talk out their feelings helps alleviate some of their guilt.

Most families dread telling siblings about the imminence of the impending death. They fear the reaction that the news will provoke—physical violence, emotional outbursts, or other manifestations of grief. Many parents predict how each sibling will react—some violently, some with hostility, some by withdrawal. Some children have no reactions at all, or try to support the parents, which may increase the parents' guilt and frustration. It is important that the siblings not be excluded at this time. It is easier to involve them if they have been an active part of the family from the beginning. The parents need to be forewarned that inclusion is painful for the siblings but that exclusion is even more so. Both parents and children need to express their feelings rather than to protect one another.

Siblings and parents need a great deal of support as the death approaches. Some siblings prefer to talk to members of the staff than to their grief-stricken parents. This is one more reason why rapport with the entire family should be made early and continued throughout the illness. Adolescent siblings have a particularly difficult time. Visiting should not be restricted, but discretion should be used. Limiting the number of visitors can be a relief to both the family and the sick child.

Most of the fears of the family and child concern the child's physical needs being met. It is important that the education of families and patients should not end when the terminal period approaches. It should be remembered also that the child may need information of a different kind from that given to his parents.

The Child's Alertness, Awareness, and State of Consciousness

Most families are greatly concerned about the child's knowing that he is dying. His level of consciousness can be assessed neurologically, but his awareness is more difficult to evaluate. Restlessness and moaning may be related more to his level of consciousness or oxygen level than to pain or fighting impending death. Parents may be embarrassed and confused over the child's disorientation. The staff and family need to be alert to what is said around the child's bed, regardless of his level of consciousness. The staff and particularly the nurses can be the role models for the proper behavior. The family and staff should continue to talk to the child and to touch him even if he is comatose, since his level of awareness may be greater than it appears. This is not to give false hope to the family but to maintain the child's dignity.

The child's questions should be answered on his own level and honestly. It is important to listen to what the child is saying. Adults often jump in with answers to questions they think the child is asking. Answers that are short, concise, and open-ended are the most appropriate. If the questions is not answerable, the child should honestly be told so. The dying child should be free to be himself and to share himself as openly as possible. This openness allows for more closeness than the family and child may have thought possible. After the death many parents are grateful that the child was able to share their love and goodbyes. One parent said several months after the death:

> I thought the staff was crazy and cruel to encourage us to talk so openly. I didn't think he had such intense love and understanding of life and us. It was the greatest gift he could have given us. We cried together and we realized he really wasn't afraid to die. He was more worried how we'd do after his death.

Vital Signs

Vital signs may or may not be taken during the terminal period. The practice of taking them is sometimes discontinued at the request of family and/or medical staff. Some parents do not want their child bothered any more, feeling that enough has been done. Others want the staff's reassurance that nothing is being overlooked. The family should always be informed of changes in routine. The decision to discontinue taking vital signs or to take them only infrequently does not mean abandonment by the staff. It allows a quiet, natural death, free of distractions and interruptions for the child and family. The child's care remains a priority.

The time spent taking vital signs allows contact and communication with the child. He is probably quite used to these procedures and therefore they should not be frightening to him. When the monitoring is increased, one can reassure an older child with, "Toby, Dr. Mike wants me to listen to your heart every half hour." A younger child may be told, "Dr. Mike wants me to listen to your heart when the clock is at 3 and 9 or 6 and 12. This gives me more time with you. I love you and being with you. I know it's scary to be sick. I'll answer any questions you have. You tell me what makes it easier." Reassurances of this kind must be sincere and promises carried out. The very sick, partially alert, or very young child may have to be told what is happening in stages. The frequent care needed may allow the family a time away from the child. The staff should not become too dependent upon monitoring equipment and abandon the child and family.

Respiratory Needs

Most families are afraid their child will choke, suffocate, or fight for breath at the time of death. Explaining the changes that may take place is important. The child's color, sounds of stridor, pulmonary edema, or change in respiratory patterns should be explained to allay as many fears as possible. An airway or respirator may or may not be used depending upon the needs and condition of the child. For example, an endotracheal (ET) tube is contraindicated in cases of thrombocytopenia. If an ET tube is in place, the family needs the reassurance that although their child cannot talk, they can still talk to him and touch him. The respirator has peculiar sounds, signals, lights, and buttons that may be frightening without explanations.

The child may be allowed to lie on the parent's lap instead of on a pillow to maintain a straight airway. The parents should not be left alone at this time. They should be told that the child could die in their arms. They need to be reassured that they will not cause his death.

Equipment

Machinery and equipment should never take the place of human caring, even though they are an important and necessary part of medical care. Machines and monitors must be used in conjunction with personal assessment of the patient and family. Simple explanations and anticipatory education can help alleviate the fears of the child and family regarding frightening pieces of equipment. For example, the changes in an oscilloscope or the alarm on an apneic monitor may only mean that the child has moved or that a lead has become loose, and *not* that he has had a respiratory or cardiac arrest. Families and staff sometimes place blind faith in the miracles of machines and technology, denying the reality that the child is dying.

Drainage

Drainage is a frequent problem. The odor, appearance, consistency, and sounds of different kinds of drainage can haunt the family long after the death. The most common types of drainage are serous, bleeding, mucous, or purulent (from skin, gastrointestinal, pulmonary, nasal-oral, eyes, ears, via incisions, arterial or venous lines, lumbar and/or venipunctures) in addition to drainage as a result of incontinency, emesis, etc.

Constant nursing care is necessary to keep the child clean and to provide adequate skin care. The family needs explanations for the cause and results of the drainages. Some are self-explanatory, but when a family is in acute grief nothing should be taken for granted. The bright red drainage from the chest tube may make the parents believe that their child is bleeding to death or may drown in his own secretions if they do not understand the placement and functions of the tube; naso-gastric drainage may appear as diarrhea to the family. The possibility of incontinent, nasal, and oral drainage at death should be anticipated and explained to the family. When the staff display confidence, understanding, and lack of fear or disgust, they give the family an appropriate role model to follow.

Alleviation of Pain

The fear most often mentioned by families and children concerns the amount and type of pain the child must endure in the course of the illness and particularly at the time of death. Parents may perceive pain in their child that the staff are unable to observe and may demand that the child's discomfort be alleviated. If the staff disagree with the parents' assessment, strife and tension will probably ensue. "You don't know my child like I know my child." The child's anxiety level and pain can well increase as a direct result of such confrontations.

Often, the child hides his pain in front of the staff; he may do so for fear of medications, bad-tasting analgesics, or nauseating side effects, or to manipulate the parents in order to gain attention, or because he is angry. Each of these possibilities must be evaluated. Continuity of care can be a great help, but may also lead to complacency, fatigue, and hostility on the part of the staff. It may be the nursing staff who must fight to get more adequate analgesics when the physician and/or family fears addiction. If the situation is carefully assessed, nurses will not be caught in the middle of such disputes.

The open setting allows the child and family to express their fears and uncertainties. Again, the value of anticipatory education cannot be overestimated. The staff should explain, for instance, that although starting an IV may be painful, it allows medications to be given more efficiently and monitored more closely; similarly, a spinal tap is painful, but the resulting alleviation of increased intracranial pressure makes it worth doing.

Asking the child which mode of medication he prefers, if there is a choice, may be of help. He may prefer an oral route to an intramuscular, or want the medication masked by his chosen method. If it is easier for the child to take a bad-tasting medication with orange sherbet, then he should be given orange sherbet—the staff's sugar water or cherry syrup does not meet his needs. Taking a piece of ice before a bad-tasting medication is a way to temporarily decrease the sensitivity of taste buds. One can offer a child an antiemetic (oral or suppository) a short time before medications that induce nausea and vomiting. Many children refuse suppositories, however, and their wishes should be respected whenever possible.

The family should be kept informed of the name of the medication, the dose, and the frequency. This alleviates anxiety when the child is being cared for by a staff member who is unfamiliar with him. For example, on a busy night in the emergency room when speed is essential, "Demerol 50 mg" or "codeine 30 mg every 4 to 6 hours" are more helpful answers to questions about medication than "the little white pill." When the child and family know their needs will be met to the best of the staff's ability, the need for medication may decrease. We in nursing can now go beyond saying "Doctor says." Explaining the side effects, mode of administration, and absorption rate to patients allows them to understand that a medication cannot be given more frequently than, say, every 4 to 6 hours. In the health care profession, we sometimes become too dependent upon medication to alleviate pain when other modes of therapy and nursing care may be more effective, e.g., changing position, suctioning, bathing, or modifying fluid intake. Providing a change of scene, listening to anxieties, anticipating needs, answering lights promptly, or checking on the patient and family *between* their calls for help are effective ways of making patients more comfortable.

To anticipate the needs of the child, one may give an analgesic before painful procedures. This tells the child and family that the procedure will be made easier, permitting more cooperation and greater tolerance of the discomfort involved. A simple explanation is adequate; "This will help your back to feel better when I help you with your bath." "This medicine will make it more fun to ride in the halls." "You may be a little sleepy after the medicine but mommy and daddy and I will be with you." "This will numb your skin so you don't feel the pain." This tells the child that the procedure is uncomfortable, but that everything possible will be done to alleviate the discomfort.

Phrases such as "deadening" or "put to sleep" have inappropriate connotations for the child. For instance, when the aging family dog was put to sleep, he never came home again or else the family buried him in the backyard; and people do "get dead" when they get shot on TV.

When analgesics are given to them promptly, many children will not require medication as often. When a child knows that her light will be answered promptly and that she will be checked on regularly, will feel less need to hoard medications or to demand them in advance. When a delay does take place, she can understand and tolerate it better.

We have made little progress if patients have to die in pain in this age of advanced technology. Lack of care and concern for the dying person destroys his dignity and self-respect.

Elimination Needs

One of the basic functions of life—elimination—is often overlooked when a child has a terminal illness. Anticipation of the child's elimination needs is essential. Side effects from therapy, positioning, or the illness itself may add to the problems of elimination. The 3- or 4-year-old is mortified when on admission he is placed in diapers. After all his efforts to become independent and free from wet pants, he is again put into a position of dependency and treated as an infant. There may be times when incontinency requires a type of diapering even for an adolescent. Explanations such as the following can help the embarrassed child deal with incontinency: "John, we won't have to move you so often when we do this." "A Chux will help, then you don't have to have the pins or have the entire bed changed so often. I know that jars you and I don't like to have you hurt." "The medicine (or infection) makes your bowels loose. It's not your fault." "We can't use the bedpan right now, so this is the way we'll help you."

A urinary catheter may be necessary in cases of continual incontinence, paralysis or injury, or after surgery. Most children find catheters not only uncomfortable but embarrassing and cumbersome. The school age child and adolescent think that "everybody is looking at my pee." They often want the bag out of sight.

If the child's bowels must be controlled by a regime of enemas or suppositories, a time that is convenient for him (either before or after seeing visitors) should be worked out in the nursing care plan. Many children refuse visitors out of embarrassment. The adolescent prefers a girlfriend or boyfriend not to visit if the odor of defecation becomes obvious during the visit. The younger child generally wants his mother to change him, while the older child may prefer a member of the staff. The child's body image and ego can be destroyed by remarks, looks of disgust, or impatience with his incontinence. The nurse should answer his call light promptly and empty his bedpan or urinal quickly.

Nutritional Needs

The type of illness, the therapy used, and the child's age and condition may make nutrition a special problem in nursing care. Most children cannot be convinced that eating will make them better. A child may have eaten well one day and find herself feeling worse the next. Fluids will be intolerable to a child who vomits three times as much as her intake. The bitter, lasting taste of medication can also be a detriment to a child's appetite. Often, frozen dinners, hamburgers with french fries, or a special dinner brought from home will be far more appealing than hospital fare, which is presented at bizarre times of day. What toddler ever waited until 8:30 or 9 a.m. to eat his breakfast, or until 1 or 1:30 p.m. for lunch? What adolescent likes to eat dinner at 4:30 or 5 p.m.? The serving provided are equivalent to an appetizer for the adolescent, while they look like a mountain of food to the preschooler. Moreover, it is impossible to force any sick, anorectic child to eat.

Allowing home foods and snacks and respecting likes and dislikes whenever possible are good ways to increase the child's food intake. Other inducements include letting the child use a favorite mug or glass from home, decorating a cup for him, or having eating contests giving stars for each ounce taken. The child should be given choices, and offered small servings that he can manage successfully. A tactful and flexible approach can help avoid temper tantrums and vomiting induced by anxiety or anger.

Topical anesthetics are often necessary for children who have gastrointestinal ulcers following chemotherapy or infections. In this situation, cold drinks may be more tolerable than hot ones to some children, or vice versa. One Mexican child could tolerate tacos but consistently vomited "those dumb American crackers!" Another child suffering from hypokalemia had vomited all the oral potassium given her and had reached the limits of intravenous treatment. It was found possible to increase her oral intake of potassium by giving her popcorn with salt substitute, which has a potassium base.

Refusing food and fluids can also be a form of manipulation. The child soon realizes that it is more effective than temper tantrums in getting family and staff aroused. One family convinced their child to eat by giving him a dollar for each tidbit swallowed. The tidbits got smaller and smaller, and the parents became more desperate. The grandparents then offered 5 dollars apiece! The child was caught sneaking food by a staff member. "Listen, I got it made," the boy said. "At this rate, I'll be rich, but I'm starving. But they can't find out now I don't mind eating. Then I'd be sunk." Obviously, the less attention that is given to lack of appetite, the less stress and strain there will be on all concerned.

Sleep and Rest

The child's normal sleep patterns can be determined from the patient history, although they will obviously change as the condition of the child changes. The adolescent may have not been in bed at 9 p.m. since he was 10 months old. The toddler may be used to sleeping with a stuffed toy or to hearing the cries of a smaller sibling, and to him the silence can be deafening. On the other hand, for a child used to the quietness of a countryside, the noise of the city hospital can prevent sleep. Night lights may cause sleeplessness for some, but take away the fears of what lurks behind the mysterious doors of a medical center for others.

A school-age or adolescent child may be embarrassed or frightened if a parent insists on sleeping in the same room. This tells some children they are dying, and quickly. Some children prefer a cool to a warm room, some the reverse. Factors such as lack of privacy, awkward positioning, the sounds of the monitoring equipment, the discomfort of an IV, pain, and fear are deterrents to sleep. The child's individual needs and preferences must be assessed so that he or she can be helped to sleep or rest as comfortably as possible.

Temperature Control

Many children are faced with serious or even life-threatening infections resulting from the disease, trauma, therapy, or a debilitated state. The child who is granulocytopenic, for example, is seriously threatened by infection. Often the high fevers cannot be controlled by medication (antipyretics and/or antibiotics). Sponging and cooling blankets, if inappropriately used, may make temperatures increase or decrease too rapidly causing convulsions and resulting in discomfort and increased anxiety for the child and family. Shivering will cause the temperature to rise. The child on the cooling blanket needs to be turned frequently. He or she can be extremely uncomfortable if the affected area is exposed to the low temperatures for extended lengths of time. Monitoring fluid intake is important.

Seizure Control

A child's seizure can be almost as frightening to a family as bleeding and death itself. There are many causes for seizures. A child may experience seizures throughout the course of the illness or only at the terminal period. Some children never have to face them. Explanations and anticipatory guidance are important once again. Calmness on the part of the staff can help avoid panic when a seizure occurs. Many uninformed parents have commented that when they saw a padded tongue blade or airway taped to the head of the child's bed, they feared that the staff would use them to silence parents or child if they said the wrong thing. A simple explanation could have settled their fears regarding both the seizures and the equipment.

Medications

Nurses are frequently faced with the problem of a child's refusal to take medication. The family may already have found ways of dealing with the child's reluctance, so nurses should be willing to listen and observe. A child may be too embarrassed to tell parents and staff that he cannot swallow pills, no matter what the size or shape. Ridiculing him or demanding that he swallow a pill only adds to the child's embarrassment and makes it more likely that he will dispose of the medication. It is far easier and much more therapeutic to crush a pill, or to mix a capsule with ice cream, than to allow the intact oral medication (and the money it cost) to go down the drain.

Compliance is a continuing problem, and should never be taken for granted.

There are many reasons why a child may not cooperate: side effects, cost of medications, unpleasant mode of administration, unawareness of the importance of continuing, prescriptions that are not written for renewal, lost or misplaced drugs. The list is as varied as the individuals. Perhaps the most common reason— "I forgot"—is the most valid.

The stress of the illness may cause the child and family to use medications incorrectly. One young girl took her medication daily before a big social event, instead of twice weekly. She ended up with a serious case of toxicity *and* missed the event. Parents may under- or overdose due to preoccupation, grief, anxiety, misunderstanding, a former routine, or newness of administration. "I took it for granted that this new drug would be given the same way as his last one. I didn't even read the label. The doctor didn't say. He just said it was a similar drug, but better, with fewer side effects, and I was thrilled," cried a mother who had overdosed her child with a new medication. "I wondered why the pill was a different color and size. I called the pharmacist and he said I had the right prescription. The next day he called and said the prescription had been filled wrong. It was twice the dose she was to get. No wonder her pain decreased so rapidly, and she slept so much."

The child and parents who live with illness become experienced; even so, they sometimes try to assume too much responsibility. "I decided if two was a good dose, then three or four would be even better. I had hoped that would cure him, not make him so sick," remarked a desperate mother.

Since we are dealing with life-and-death measures, which often include chemotherapy with extremely toxic effects, the role of medication cannot be taken lightly. The family and child faced with anger and hostility because they have forgotten (or discontinued) therapy may end up lying, or refusing to resume therapy to prove how well the child can do without it. Some families have religious reasons for not taking prescribed medications.

The desperate search for a cure, particularly during the terminal phase, may lead some families to quackery and illegal therapy. No family is immune from at least thinking about such alternatives when conventional and experimental therapy have failed. These are families of dying children, who will go to almost any lengths to prolong their child's life or to alleviate his pain. These "cures" are enticing because they have no side effects, while the conventional therapy that is failing may have serious, often devastating ones.

The observant nurse can often pick up discrepancies while she is taking the history. Comments from the family about the time and manner of taking the drug and the necessity for prescription renewals often provide clues. Blood or urine levels may reveal a decrease or overdose or the discontinuation of therapy.

Procedures

The procedures a dying child has to undergo are, at the very least, uncomfortable and frequently painful. It is no wonder that the child dreads these so-called routine procedures. Nevertheless, it is not feasible to heed all the child's directions, refusals, or demands. This should be made clear to the child and family at the outset. Discretion should be used as to when and how treatments should be carried out. For example, to take the preschooler away from his mother while he is resting, or to disrupt a meal to perform painful, non-emergency procedures, is thoughtless and inconsiderate. The regime of the hospital is routine to the staff, but not to the child and his family.

Knowing what to expect can help the child, but it may also increase anxiety. Fear of the known is as real as fear of the unknown. Nurses should remember that children are often embarrassed about their lack of cooperation and their "bad" behavior during procedures. Adolescents, in particular, will rarely admit to the staff their embarrassment over crying and not cooperating. They may, however, confide in an empathetic staff member, and many request that their favorite staff member be with them at such times. One adolescent boy told a favorite nurse after a great commotion during a painful, long procedure:

> I guess I really did act like an idiot, but those damn needles really hurt.
>
> It makes me so mad when they keep saying I'm acting like a baby. I already know I am. I know I look like a fool. I can't help it. I know they can't stand me. I can't stand them, either. They're so smug with all those remarks. I wish *they* had had hundred of sticks. Please be with me when you can.

The child needs to know that the procedure has to be done and that with his cooperation it will be done as quickly and as painlessly as possible. Children can accept pain more readily from staff they trust and like. "I know you hate to stick me 'cause I'm so neat, but I'd rather have you [the nurse] do it than those ugly men [the residents]. You really like me. I'll holler but I'll try to hold still," said a knowing 9-year-old. "Just get it over with instead of clowning around," was the request of an 11-year-old. Staff should at all costs avoid lies or threats. Nor should they allow parents to threaten the child with statements such as "I'll have the nurse or doctor give you a shot if you are bad." If parents *have* made such threats it should be made clear immediately in front of the parents and child that the health care team does not punish children with painful procedures.

Family Participation

No family should be forced to care for their child during crucial periods. However, the child belongs to the family, and when feasible and applicable they have the right to help in his or her care. A takeover by staff can communicate nonverbally, and sometimes verbally, that the parents are incompetent. This is painful for the family, for most are terribly insecure in the role of parents of a dying child, a role one never gets used to. The responsibilities only increase as the terminal phase progresses.

Most parents try extremely hard to do the right thing. They want to provide care that is as painless as possible for their child. They resent staff who reject their contributions. Some, however, are relieved when others take over the care, particularly during the terminal phase, by which time most familes are exhausted physically and emotionally.

The observant staff can pick up clues about the parents' attitudes. "I know you know the best way to care for Teddy," may be a way of saying, "I'm afraid of taking care of him," or "I'm so tired." It may also be a test to see if the staff will trust the parent with the care of the child. The family may need an "out" to relieve them of the continual care of the sick child. They may be subtly begging someone to take over the heavy responsibilities they have carried for years. In any case, it is important for both child and family that the health care providers allow them to be part of the team. Each family has to be treated individually. A mother may need permission to get away from her child, while a father may want to become more directly involved in the child's care. His only chance to do so may be during hospitalizations.

Because they have the most direct care of the child, nurses must be careful to avoid arrogating the care and affections of the child. They should not enter a contest with the parents for his attention and affection.

THE DEATH

Death comes as a shock no matter what preparation has been made for it. The staff should continue to deal honestly with the family at the time of death. Whenever possible, the family should be told the child's death is imminent. Their grief may make it difficult for them to absorb the painful reality, but this does not absolve the health care team from telling them the truth.

Although it is painful and final, the family should hear the word "death." Words such as "critical," "looks bad," and "very serious," do not convey the irreversibility of death. The family may have previously faced serious or critical situations and seen the child survive. When they are not dealt with frankly, most families complain after the death. Some may comment that they heard the word "death" and that the rest of the conversation was obliterated in the shock. "It made me think that it was really going to happen this time," remarked a father. "When the doctor said things looked really bad, it made me relive all the bad times before. It didn't register that he meant Jake would die. I probably should have known it. I guess you deny till the end unless someone shakes your tree with 'He's dying.' "

After the death, some families again prefer to be alone for a time with their child. Staff should always be close by when the families request these moments alone either before or after the death. It appears to help most families if they can see (and even touch) their child before they see him at the funeral home.

The final goodbye to the staff is often accompanied by a great deal of emotion. The removal of the child's possessions may have begun before his death or may have to be done at this time. Some families want others to do the packing. Other families prefer to do it themselves.

Chapters 10 and 11 have additional material on dealing with the child's death.

Home Death

It is becoming increasingly common, particularly among adult patients and their families, to choose to die at home. Families who decide to have their child die at home need a great deal of help. They must be carefully instructed about drainage, incontinency, control of pain or possible seizures, and about potential changes in color, respiration, alertness, and consciousness. We cannot take for granted that a family understands the problems they may encounter. The family whose child dies in the hospital knows that trained staff are always at hand. This is not the case for the family whose child dies at home. During the preparation for dismissal, the family should be asked to reiterate what they have been taught. Staff can then make sure they understand the information that is important, and give the family a chance to ask questions.

The staff should make it clear to the family that they are free to return, call, or write if they have questions, or to reverse their decision should problems arise. Asking staff for help is not a sign of failure, but a mature way of handling a very painful and delicate situation. The staff should be available at any time to offer assistance. The family should have the names and telephone numbers of the regular staff, as well as of backup staff who may be called upon when regular staff are unavailable. It should not be up to the family to track down members of the health care team when a problem arises.

Some members of the staff may feel threatened by the family's decision to take the child home. They should take care not to convey their negative feelings or to make the family feel rejected. Otherwise it may be difficult for families to reverse their decision, and they may feel trapped in a frightening situation. Making routine daily calls to the family is a particularly useful way to maintain continuous contact. The time should be adjusted for the convenience of all parties, and it is wise to set a broad period, such as between 8 a.m. and 10 a.m., to allow for busy lines, staff responsibilities, etc. The calls may be rotated among staff members, or one member may act as the liaison.

The family needs preparation for the death itself. They should be told *in writing* what to do and whom to call when the death occurs. The emotional shock of the death will make it difficult for them to remember.

When preparing the family for the child's death, the word "death" should be used. The statement: "After Jamies dies, you will need to contact _____." clearly conveys that the family has chosen to take their child home to *die*. "Any time you have questions or problems, or just need to talk, do please call me. If you'd prefer, you can come in and see me, either alone or with Pattie." This states clearly that the family is welcome to visit or call, with or without the child.

After Death

Care of the family does not end with the death of the child. Some of the most difficult times the family has to face occur after the death. The nurse who cared for the child often remains in contact, particularly if she was closely involved with the family throughout the ups and downs of the illness.

It is appropriate to visit, call, or write soon after the death, even before the funeral. This can help the family as well as allowing the nurse to begin coping with her own grief. Some nurses find themselves supporting the family, others find that the family gives *them* support, and still others find it too painful to maintain contact. A person who experiences intense grief with the death of every patient may need special help to deal with her emotions.

The duration of the postdeath follow-up depends on many factors, including time, distance, and other responsibilities. Some families never lose contact with hospital staff, while others prefer to break the ties when their mourning period is over. Families whose child did not survive the initial induction period often desire no further contact. When visiting or calling on the family, the nurse should not be afraid to talk about the child, or to refer to him by name. It helps the family to resolve their grief if they can relive the events of the child's life. In fact, one of the greatest frustrations for the family is that others do not wish to talk about the child, or to discuss his illness or death.

The nurse should be aware of the fact that some families may need referrals to ministers, counselors, family physicians, or other professionals during the postdeath period.

It is important for the entire health care team to support one another. One staff member may be grieving the loss of a favorite child just at a time when several other children are diagnosed as being fatally ill.

TEAM APPROACH

To care adequately and fully for dying children a team approach is essential. The members of the team may be drawn from many different disciplines. Ideally all specialties should be included, but this is not possible in a community hospital or even in many large medical centers. The team members need to work well with one another as well as with the house staff and nursing staff on the unit. House and nursing staff are most directly involved with patient care. In order to work well with children, health care providers must understand and like them. Being a pediatric specialist does not guarantee that one works well with children, family, and staff. The ideal team to care for the dying child is outlined in Table 4.

Table 4 The Ideal Team

A   Basic Medical Team
    1   Physicians (family practitioner, pediatrician, specialist)
    2   Psychiatrists and/or psychologists or counselors
    3   Nurses (staff, clinical specialist, and/or practitioner)
    4   Fellows (all specialties)
    5   Residents (family practice, pediatric, and specialties rotating)
    6   Laypersons (when available or applicable)

B Allied Health Care Team
  1 Social workers
  2 Respiratory therapists
  3 Occupational therapists
  4 Physical therapists
  5 Dietitians
  6 Medical technologists
  7 Technicians in specific areas
    a Hematology-oncology
    b Nephrology-dialysis
    c CV
    d Surgery
    e Radiology
    f EKG
    g EEG
    h IV
    i Orthopedics
    j Burns
    k Other
  8 Special education teachers (hospital, public, private)
  9 Radiologists
    a Diagnostic
    b Nuclear medicine
    c Radiation oncology
  10 Ministers
C Students
  1 Nursing
  2 Medical
  3 Allied health care, as mentioned in **B**
D Organizations as Extensions of Help to Family and Child
  1 SIDS
  2 Myelomeningocele Association
  3 Leukemia Society
  4 Cancer Society
  5 Parent group organizations
  6 AA
  7 Public Health Nurse Association
  8 Crippled Children's Commission
  9 March of Dimes
  10 Cystic Fibrosis Association
  11 Other
E Community Care
  1 Public agencies as in **D**
  2 Community health nurses
  3 Home visits, telephone calls, and letters
  4 Satellite clinics
  5 Support and guidance with family health care provider

Bibliography

PART ONE

Books for Children about Death

Bach, Richard: *Jonathan Livingston Seagull,* Avon, New York, 1973.

Bell, Martin: *The Way of the Wolf: The Gospel in New Images,* The Seabury Press, New York, 1961.

Blue, Rose: *Grandma Didn't Wave Back,* Franklin Watts, New York, 1972.

*Brown, Margaret Wise: *The Death Bird,* Young Scout Books, Reading, Mass., 1958.

Craven, Margaret: *I Heard an Owl Call My Name,* Doubleday, New York, 1973.

Fahs, Sophia L. and Dorothy T. Spoerl: *Beginnings: Earth, Sky, Life, Death,* Beacon Press, Boston, 1958.

*Fassler, Joan: *My Grandpa Died Today,* Behavioral Publications, New York, 1971.

Gallico, Paul: *The Snow Goose,* Alfred A. Knopf, New York, 1972.

Grollman, Earl: *Explaining Death to Children,* Beacon Press, Boston, 1967.

Grollman, Earl: *Talking about Death: A Dialog Between Parent and Child,* Beacon Press, Boston, 1969.

*Highly recommended

*Harris, Audrey: *Why Did He Die?* Lerner Publishing, No. Minneapolis, Minn., 1965.

*Kavannaugh, James: *Celebrate the Sun,* Nash Publishing, Los Angeles, 1973.

Langone, John: *Death Is a Noun,* Little, Brown, Boston, 1972.

*Lee, Virginia: *The Magic Moth,* The Seabury Press, New York, 1972.

*Little, Jean: *Home from Far,* Little, Brown, Boston, 1965.

Miles, Mishka: *Annie and the Old One,* Little, Brown, Boston, 1971.

*Orgel, Doris: *Mulberry Music,* Harper & Row, New York, 1971.

Patterbaum, Gerald: *Thank God for Circles,* Augsburg Publishing, Minneapolis, Minn., 1971.

Schecter, Ben: *Across the Meadow,* Doubleday, New York, 1973.

*Silverstein, Shel: *The Giving Tree,* Harper & Row, New York, 1964.

Smith, Doris B.: *Taste of Blackberries,* T. Y. Crowell, New York, 1973.

Stein, Sara Bonnett: *About Dying: An Open Family Book for Parents and Children Together,* Walker, New York, 1974.

*Viorst, Judith: *The Tenth Good Thing about Barney,* Atheneum, New York, 1971.

*Warburg, Sandol Stoddard: *Growing Time,* Houghton Mifflin, Boston, 1969.

*Williams, Margery: *The Velveteen Rabbit,* Doubleday, New York, 1958.

Zin, Herbert S. and Sonia Bleecker: *Life and Death,* William Morrow, New York, 1970.

General

Benoliel, Jeanne Quint: "The Terminally Ill Child," in Gladys Scipien et al. (eds.), *Comprehensive Pediatric Nursing,* McGraw-Hill, New York, 1975, pp. 423–440.

Bergmann, Thesi: *Children in the Hospital,* International Universities Press, New York, 1965.

Bigner, Jerry J.: "The School Age Child—6 to 12 Years," in Gladys Scipien et al. (eds.), *Comprehensive Pediatric Nursing,* McGraw-Hill, New York, 1975, pp. 156–167.

Binger, C. M. et al.: "Childhood Leukemia: Emotional Impact on Patient and Family," *The New England Journal of Medicine,* vol. 280, no. 8, pp. 414–418, February 20, 1969.

Branson, Helen Kitchen: "The Dying Child," *Bedside Nurse,* vol. 5, no. 2, pp. 11–15, February 1972.

Buhrmann, M. V.: "The Dying Child," *South African Medical Journal,* vol. 47, no. 25, pp. 1114–1116, June 30, 1973.

Burgert, E. O., Jr.: "Psychological Management of Children with Cancer and of Their Families," *Paediatrician,* vol. 1, no. 1, pp. 311–318, 1972–1973.

†Buscaglia, Leo: *The Disabled and Their Parents: A Counseling Challenge,* Charles B. Slack, Thorofare, N. J., 1975.

*Highly recommended
†Of interest to parents

Byers, Mary Lou: "The Hospitalized Adolescent," *Nursing Outlook,* vol. 15, no. 8, pp. 32–34, August 1967.

Carey, William B. and Maarten S. Sibinga: "Avoiding Pediatric Pathogenesis in the Management of Acute Minor Illness," *Pediatrics,* vol. 49, no. 4, pp. 553–562, April 1972.

Clancy, Barbara J. and Jeanne Schoot: "The Infant—1 to 12 Months," in *Comprehensive Pediatric Nursing,* Gladys Scipien et al. (eds.), McGraw-Hill, New York, 1975, pp. 115–123.

Cook, Sarah L. Sheets et al.: *Children and Dying,* Health Sciences, New York, 1973.

Cragg, Catherine E.: "The Child with Leukemia," *The Canadian Nurse,* vol. 65, no. 10, pp. 30–34, October 1969.

Craven, Ruth F. and Benita H. Sharp: "The Effects of Illness on Family Functions," *Nursing Forum,* vol. 11, no. 2, pp. 187–193, 1972.

Cyphert, Frederick R.: "Back to School for the Child with Cancer," *The Journal of School Health,* vol. 43, no. 4, pp. 215–217, April 1973.

Danilowica, Delores A. and H. Paul Gabriel: "Death in Childhood," *The Canadian Medical Association Journal,* vol. 98, no. 20, pp. 967–969, May 18, 1968.

Danilowica, Delores A. and H. Paul Gabriel: "Post-Operative Reactions in Children: 'Normal' and 'Abnormal' Responses after Cardiac Surgery," *American Journal of Psychiatry,* vol. 128, no. 2, pp. 77–80, August 1971.

Debuskey, Matthew and Robert H. Dombro: *The Chronically Ill Child and His Family,* Charles C Thomas, Springfield, Ill., 1970.

Duffy, John C.: "Emotional Reactions of Children to Hospitalization," *Minnesota Medicine,* vol. 55, no. 12, pp. 1168–1170, December 1972.

Duran, Maria Tortoreto: "Family-Centered Care and the Adolescent's Quest for Self-Identity," *Nursing Clinics of North America,* vol. 7, no. 1, pp. 65–73, March 1972.

Erickson, Florence H.: "Helping the Sick Child Maintain Behavioral Control," *Nursing Clinics of North America,* vol. 2, no. 4, pp. 695–703, December 1967.

Erickson, Florence H.: "Stress in the Pediatric Ward," *Maternal-Child Nursing Journal,* vol. 1, no. 2, pp. 113–116, Summer 1972.

Fond, Karen Ikuno: "Dealing with Death and Dying Through Family-Centered Care," *Nursing Clinics of North America,* vol. 7, no. 1, pp. 53–64, March 1972.

Fraiberg, Selma H.: *The Magic Years,* Scribner's, New York, 1959.

Furth, Gregory: "Impromptu Paintings by Terminally Ill, Hospitalized and Healthy Children: What We Can Learn from Them," Dissertation, Ohio State University, 1973.

†Fynn: *Mister God, This Is Anna,* Holt, Rinehart and Winston, New York, 1974.

Greene, Patricia: "The Child with Leukemia in the Classroom," *American Journal of Nursing,* vol. 75, no. 1, pp. 86–87, January 1975.

†Of interest to parents

Griffin, Caryl P. and Trude R. Aufhauser: "Don't Let Them Hurt Me," *AORN Journal*, vol. 17, no. 5, pp. 59–65, May 1973.

†Grollman, Earl A.: *Explaining Death to Children*, Beacon Press, Boston, 1967.

†Grollman, Earl A.: *Talking about Death: A Dialogue Between Parent and Child*, Beacon Press, Boston, 1970.

Gyulay, Jo-Eileen: "Interactions of Terminally Ill Children and Their Parents," in *A.N.A. Clinical Sessions*, Appleton-Century-Crofts, New York, 1974, pp. 92–98.

Hyman, Martin D.: "Disability and Patients' Perceptions of Preferential Treatment: Some Preliminary Findings," *Journal of Chronic Diseases*, vol. 24, pp. 329–341, 1971.

Isler, Charlotte: "The Cancer Nurses: Part 2. Care of the Pediatric Patient with Leukemia," *R.N.*, vol. 35, pp. 30–35, April 1972.

†Jackson, Edgar N.: *Telling a Child about Death*, Hawthorn Books, New York, 1965.

Jersild, Arthur T.: *The Psychology of Adolescence*, Macmillan, New York, 1963.

Kaplan, David M. et al.: "School Management of the Seriously Ill Child," *The Journal of School Health*, vol. 44, no. 5, pp. 250–254, May 1974.

Karon, Myron: "The Physician and the Adolescent with Cancer," *Pediatric Clinics of North America*, vol. 20, no. 4, pp. 965–969, November 1973.

Karon, Myron and Joel Vernick: "Approach to the Emotional Support of Fatally Ill Children," *Clinical Pediatrics*, vol. 7, no. 5, pp. 274–280, May 1968.

Kaufman, Richard V.: "Body-Image Changes in Physically Ill Teen-Agers," *Journal of American Academy of Child Psychiatry*, vol. 11, pp. 157–170, January 1972.

Kikuchi, June: "A Leukemia Adolescent's Verbalization about Dying," *Maternal-Child Nursing Journal*, vol. 1, no. 3, pp. 259–264, Fall 1972.

†Klein, Norma: *Sunshine*, Avon, New York, 1974.

Korsch, Barbara M. et al.: "Experiences with Children and Their Families During Extended Hemodialysis and Kidney Transplantation," *Pediatric Clinics of North America*, vol. 18, no. 2, pp. 625–637, May 1971.

Kuneman, Lucy: "Some Factors Influencing a Young Child's Mastery of Hospitalization," *Nursing Clinics of North America*, vol. 7, no. 1, pp. 13–26, March 1972.

Lacasse, Christine Mitchell: "A Dying Adolescent," *American Journal of Nursing*, vol. 75, no. 3, pp. 433–434, March 1975.

Lansky, Shirley B. et al.: "School Phobia in Children with Malignant Neoplasma," *American Journal of Diseases of Children*, vol. 129, pp. 42–46, January 1975.

Lansky, Shirley B. et al.: "A Team Approach to Coping with Cancer," in Joseph W. Cullen et al. (eds.), *Cancer: The Behavioral Dimensions*, National Cancer Institute Monograph, Raven Press, New York, 1976, pp. 295–308.

†Levit, Rose: *Ellen: A Short Life Long Remembered*, Bantam, New York, 1974.

Linde, Leonard M. and Shirley D. Linde: "Emotional Factors of Pediatric Patients in Cardiac Surgery," *AORN Journal*, vol. 18, no. 1, pp. 95–99, July 1973.

Lowenberg, June S.: "The Coping Behaviors of Fatally Ill Adolescents and Their Parents," *Nursing Forum*, vol. 9, no. 3, pp. 269–287, 1970.

†Of interest to parents

Lowenstein, Harold: "The Handling of Distress," *Nursing Times,* vol. 58, pp. 1363–1364, November 26, 1972.

Lucente, Frank E.: "Psychological Problems in Otolaryngology," *Laryngoscope,* vol. 83, no. 10, pp. 1684–1689, October 1973.

†Lund, Doris: *Eric,* Dell, New York, 1974.

Mason, Edward A.: "The Hospitalized Child—His Emotional Needs," *The New England Journal of Medicine,* vol. 272, no. 8, pp. 406–414, February 25, 1965.

Mattsson, Ake: "Long-Term Physical Illness in Childhood: A Challenge to Psychosocial Adaptation," *Pediatrics,* vol. 50, no. 5, pp. 801–811, November 1972.

Maxwell, Sister Marie Bernadette: "A Terminally Ill Adolescent and Her Family," *American Journal of Nursing,* vol. 72, no. 5, pp. 925–927, May 1972.

Meyer, Herbert L.: "Predictable Problems of Hospitalized Adolescents," *American Journal of Nursing,* vol. 69, no. 3, pp. 525–528, March 1969.

Miya, Trudy M.: "The Child's Perception of Death," *Nursing Forum,* vol. 11, no. 2, pp. 215–220, 1972.

Mussen, Paul Henry et al.: *Child Development and Personality,* Harper & Row, New York, 1956.

Nahigian, Eileen Gallagher: "The Preschooler—3 to 5 Years" in Gladys Scipien et al. (eds.), *Comprehensive Pediatric Nursing,* McGraw-Hill, New York, 1975, pp. 139–155.

Newcome, Barbara: "Analysis of Behavior in a Terminally Ill Child," *Maternal-Child Nursing Journal,* vol. 2, no. 3, pp. 157–165, Fall 1973.

Nordan, Robert et al.: "Return to the Land of the Living: An Approach to the Problem of Chronic Hemodialysis," *Pediatrics,* vol. 48, no. 6, pp. 939–945, December 1971.

Northrup, Fran C.: "The Dying Child," *American Journal of Nursing,* vol. 74, no. 6, pp. 1066–1068, June 1974.

Nover, Robert A.: "Pain and the Burned Child," *American Journal of Academic Child Psychiatry,* vol. 12, no. 3, pp. 499–505, July 1973.

Oates, R. K.: "A Home Care Scheme for Sick Children," *The Medical Journal of Australia,* vol. 2, no. 14, pp. 698–701, October 6, 1973.

Oraftik, Nancy: "Only Time to Touch," *Nursing Forum,* vol. 11, no. 2, pp. 205–213, 1972.

Quinby, Susan and Norman R. Bernstein: "Identity Problems and the Adaptation of Nurses to Severely Burned Children," *American Journal of Psychiatry,* vol. 128, no. 1, pp. 90–95, July 1971.

Ritchie, Judith: "Fantasy in Communicating Concerns about Body Integrity," *Maternal-Child Nursing Journal,* vol. 1, no. 2, pp. 117–126, Summer 1972.

Robinson, Lisa: *Psychological Aspects of the Care of Hospitalized Patients,* F. A. Davis, Philadelphia, 1972.

Schowalter, John E.: "The Child's Reaction to His Own Terminal Illness," in Bernard Schoenberg et al. (eds.), *Loss and Grief: Psychological Management in Medical Practice,* Columbia University Press, New York, 1970, pp. 51–69.

Schowalter, John E. et al.: "The Adolescent Patient's Decision to Die," *Pediatrics,* vol. 51, no. 1, pp. 97–103, January 1973.

†Of interest to parents

Schwartz, A. Herbert: "Children's Concepts of Research Hospitalization," *The New England Journal of Medicine,* vol. 287, no. 12, pp. 589–592, September 21, 1972.

Shuster, Seymour: "Dracula and Surgically Induced Trauma in Children," *British Journal of Medical Psychology,* vol. 46, pp. 259–270, 1973.

Smart, Mollie S. and Russell C. Smart: *Children: Development and Relationships,* Macmillan, New York, 1967.

Spenner, Dorothy: "A Preschool Child Copes with Hospitalization," *Maternal-Child Nursing Journal,* vol. 3, no. 1, pp. 41–48, Spring 1974.

Spinetta, John J.: "The Dying Child's Awareness of Death: A Review," *Psychological Bulletin,* vol. 81, no. 4, pp. 256–260, 1974.

Stephens, Kathleen Schmidt: "A Toddler's Separation Anxiety," *American Journal of Nursing,* vol. 73, no. 9, pp. 1553–1555, September 1973.

Sultz, Harry A. et al.: *Long-Term Childhood Illness,* University of Pittsburgh Press, Pittsburgh, 1972.

Thorp, Isobel H.: "The Toddler—1 to 3 Years," in Gladys Scipien et al. (eds.), *Comprehensive Pediatric Nursing,* McGraw-Hill, New York, 1975, pp. 124–138.

Tiedt, Eileen: "The Adolescent in the Hospital: An Identity-Resolution Approach," *Nursing Forum,* vol. 11, no. 2, pp. 120–140, 1972.

†Valens, E.G.: *The Other Side of the Mountain,* Warner, New York, 1966.

Vernick, Joel and Myron Karon: "Who's Afraid of Death on a Leukemia Ward?" *American Journal of Diseases of Children,* vol. 109, no. 5, pp. 393–397, May 1965.

Waechter, Eugenia H.: "Children's Awareness of Fatal Illness," *American Journal of Nursing,* vol. 71, no. 6, pp. 1168–1172, June 1971.

Williams, David D.: "The Neonate—Birth to One Month," in Gladys Scipien et al. (eds.), *Comprehensive Pediatric Nursing,* McGraw-Hill, New York, 1975, pp. 100–114.

Williams, Tamara: "I Found You Gun," *Maternal-Child Nursing Journal,* vol. 3, no. 3, pp. 239–244, Fall 1974.

Wolters, W. H. G. et al.: "Experiences in the Development of a Haemodialysis Centre for Children," *Journal of Psychosomatic Research,* vol. 17, no. 4, pp. 271–276, November 1973.

Yakulis, Irene M.: "Anxieties of a Fatally Ill Boy," *Maternal-Child Nursing Journal,* vol. 2, no. 2, pp. 121–128, Summer 1973.

Yaros, Patricia S.: "The Adolescent," in Gladys Scipien et al. (eds.), *Comprehensive Pediatric Nursing,* McGraw-Hill, New York, 1975, pp. 168–183.

Zeligs, Rose: "Children's Attitudes Toward Death," *Mental Hygiene,* vol. 51, no. 3, pp. 393–396, July 1967.

PARTS TWO AND THREE

General

Ablin, Arthur R. et al.: "A Conference with the Family of a Leukemic Child," *American Journal of Diseases of Children,* vol. 122, no. 4, pp. 362–364, October 1971.

†Of interest to parents

Anthony, E. James and Theresa Benedek (eds.): *Parenthood: Its Psychology and Psychopathology*, Little, Brown, Boston, 1970.

Barton, David: "Teaching Psychiatry in the Context of Dying and Death," *American Journal of Psychiatry*, vol. 130, no. 11, pp. 1290-1291, November 1973.

Barton, David et al.: "Death and Dying: A Course for Medical Students," *Journal of Medical Education*, vol. 47, no. 12, pp. 945-951, December 1972.

†Bayly, Joseph: *A View from a Hearse*, David C. Cook, Elgin, Ill., 1969.

Beal, Susan: "The Sudden Infant Death Syndrome," *The Medical Journal of Australia*, vol. 2, no. 22, pp. 1217-1218, November 25, 1972.

Bennett, M. B.: "Care of the Dying," *South African Medical Journal*, vol. 47, no. 34, pp. 1558-1560, September 1973.

Binger, C. M. et al.: "Childhood Leukemia," *The New England Journal of Medicine*, vol. 280, no. 8, pp. 414-418, February 20, 1969.

Bonnie, Gladys N.: "Students' Reactions to Children's Deaths," *American Journal of Nursing*, vol. 67, no. 7, pp. 1439-1440, July 1967.

Braverman, Shirley J.: "Death of a Monster," *American Journal of Nursing*, vol. 69, no. 8, pp. 183-185, August 1969.

Bright, Florence: "The Pediatric Nurse and Parental Anxiety," *Nursing Forum*, vol. 4, no. 2, pp. 31-47, 1965.

Bright, Florence and Sister M. Luciana France: "The Nurse and the Terminally Ill Child," *Nursing Outlook*, vol. 15, no. 9, pp. 39-47, September 1967.

Brodie, Barbara: "The Nurse's Reaction to the Ill Child," *Nursing Clinics of North America*, vol. 1, no. 1, pp. 95-102, March 1966.

Bruce, Sylvia: "Reactions of Nurses and Mothers to Stillbirth," *Nursing Outlook*, vol. 10, no. 2, pp. 88-91, February 1962.

Buellock, Mitzie W.: "When the Baby Isn't Normal," *Medical Times*, vol. 101, no. 12, pp. 120-122, December 1973.

Burgert, E. O.: "Emotional Impact of Childhood Acute Leukemia," *Mayo Clinical Proceedings*, vol. 47, no. 4, pp. 273-277, April 1972.

Burgert, E. O.: "Psychological Management of Children with Cancer and of Their Families," *Paediatrician*, pp. 311-318, 1972-1973.

†Buscaglia, Leo: *Love*, Charles B. Slack, Thorofare, N.J., 1972.

Buxbaum, Rev. Robert E.: "Initial Responses to Grief and the Physician's Problems and Opportunities," *Texas Medicine*, vol. 70, no. 2, pp. 94-98, February 1974.

Carlozzi, Carl G.: *Death and the Contemporary Man: The Crisis of Terminal Illness*, William B. Eeromans, Grand Rapids, Michigan, 1968.

Caughill, Rita E.: *The Dying Patient: A Supportive Approach*, Little, Brown, Boston, 1976.

Chodoff, Paul et al.: "Stress, Defenses and Coping Behavior: Observations in Parents of Children with Malignant Disease," *American Journal of Psychiatry*, vol. 120, no. 8, pp. 743-749, February 1964.

†Colgrove, Melba et al.: *How to Survive the Loss of a Love*, Lion Press, New York, 1976.

Craig, Yvonne: "The Care of a Dying Child—The Needs of the Nurses, the Patient and Parents," *Nursing Mirror*, pp. 14-16, September 28, 1975.

†Of interest to parents

†DeVries, Peter: *The Blood of the Lamb,* Little, Brown, Boston, 1961.

†Easson, William M.: *The Dying Child: The Management of the Child or Adolescent Who Is Dying,* Charles C Thomas, Springfield, Ill., 1970.

Easson, William M.: "The Family of the Dying Child," *Pediatric Clinics of North America,* vol. 19, no. 4, pp. 1157–1165, November 1972.

Eckstein, Herbert B.: "Severely Malformed Children," *British Medical Journal,* vol. 2, pp. 284–289, May 5, 1973.

Elfert, Helen: "The Nurse and the Grieving Parent," *The Canadian Nurse,* vol. 71, no. 2, pp. 30–31, February 1975.

Fabia, Jacqueline and Thuong Dam Thuy: "Occupation of Father at Time of Birth of Children Dying of Malignant Diseases," *British Journal of Preventive Social Medicine,* vol. 28, no. 2, pp. 98–100, 1974.

Feifel, Herman (ed.): *The Meaning of Death,* McGraw-Hill, New York, 1965.

Feifel, Herman et al.: "Death Fear in Dying Heart and Cancer Patients," *Journal of Psychosomatic Research,* vol. 17, no. 3, pp. 161–166, February 1973.

Fishman, Claire A. and Daniel B. Fishman: "Emotional, Cognitive, and Interpersonal Confrontation among Children with Birth Defects," *Child Psychiatry and Human Development,* vol. 2, no. 2, pp. 92–101, Winter 1971.

Fishman, Claire A. and Daniel B. Fishman: "Maternal Correlates of Self-Esteem and Overall Adjustment in Children with Birth Defects," *Child Psychiatry and Human Development,* vol. 1, no. 4, pp. 255–265, Summer 1971.

Fletcher, John: "Attitudes Toward Defective Newborns," *Hastings Center Studies,* vol. 2, no. 1, pp. 21–32, January 1974.

Fond, Karen Ikuno: "Dealing with Death and Dying Through Family-Centered Care," *Nursing Clinics of North America,* vol. 7, no. 1, pp. 53–64, March 1972.

Fox, Sheila: "The Death of a Child," *Nursing Times,* vol. 68, pp. 1322–1323, October 19, 1972.

Freiberg, Karen H.: "How Parents React When Their Child Is Hospitalized," *American Journal of Nursing,* vol. 72, no. 7, pp. 1270–1272, July 1972.

Fretwell, Joan E.: "A Child Dies," *Nursing Times,* vol. 69, no. 27, pp. 867–871, July 5, 1973.

Friedman, Stanford B. et al.: "Behavioral Observations on Parents Anticipating the Death of a Child," *Pediatrics,* vol. 32, no. 4, pp. 610–625, October 1963.

†Friedman, Stanford B. et al.: "Childhood Leukemia: A Pamphlet for Parents," U.S. Department of Health, Education and Welfare, National Institute of Health, DHEW Publication (NIH) 72–212, revised 1972.

Fulton, Robert: *Death and Identity,* John Wiley and Sons, New York, 1965.

Furman, Robert A.: "The Child's Reaction to Death in the Family," in Bernard Schoenberg et al. (eds.), *Loss and Grief: Psychological Management in Medical Practice,* Columbia University Press, New York, 1970, pp. 70–86.

Galiardi, Diane and Margaret Shandor Miles: "Interactions Between Two Mothers of Children Suffering from Incurable Cancer," *Nursing Clinics of North America,* vol. 4, no. 1, pp. 89–100, March 1969.

Geis, Dorothy P.: "Mothers' Perceptions of Care Given Their Dying Children," *American Journal of Nursing,* vol. 65, no. 2, pp. 105–107, February 1965.

†Of interest to parents

Gillon, Janet E.: "Family Stresses When a Child Has Congenital Heart Disease," *Maternal-Child Nursing Journal,* vol. 1, no. 3, pp. 265–272, Fall 1972.

Glaser, Barney G. and Anselm L. Strauss: *Awareness of Dying,* Aldine, Chicago, 1965.

Glaser, Barney G. and Anselm L. Strauss: "The Social Loss of Dying Patients," *American Journal of Nursing,* vol. 64, no. 6, pp. 119–121, June 1964.

Glaser, Barney G. and Anselm L. Strauss: *Time for Dying,* Aldine, Chicago, 1968.

Glasser, Ronald J.: *Ward 402,* George Braziller, New York, 1973.

Goldfogel, Linda: "Working with the Parent of a Dying Child," *American Journal of Nursing,* vol. 70, no. 8, pp. 1675–1679, August 1970.

Gould, Richard K. and Michael B. Rothenberg: "The Chronically Ill Child Facing Death—How Can the Pediatrician Help?" *Clinical Pediatrics,* vol. 12, no. 7, pp. 447–449, July 1973.

Green, Morris and Albert J. Solnit: "Reactions to the Threatened Loss of a Child: A Vulnerable Child Syndrome," *Pediatrics,* vol. 34, no. 1, pp. 58–66, July 1964.

†Grollman, Earl A. (ed.): *Concerning Death: A Practical Guide for the Living,* Beacon Press, Boston, 1974.

Guimond, Joyce: "We Knew Our Child Was Dying," *American Journal of Nursing,* vol. 74, no. 2, pp. 248–249, February 1974.

Gyulay, Jo-Eileen: "Dealing with the Family of the Dying Child," *Issues in Comprehensive Pediatric Nursing,* vol. 1, no. 3, pp. 16–22, September-October 1976.

Gyulay, Jo-Eileen: "The Forgotten Grievers," *American Journal of Nursing,* vol. 75, no. 9, pp. 1476–1479, September 1975.

Gyulay, Jo-Eileen and Margaret Shandor Miles: "The Family with a Terminally Ill Child," in Debra Hymovich and Martha Barnard (eds.), *Family Health Care,* McGraw-Hill, New York, 1973, pp. 439–458.

Hendin, David: *Death as a Fact of Life,* Warner, New York, 1974.

Hinton, John: *Dying,* Penguin, Baltimore, 1974.

Hinton, John: "The Psychiatry of Terminal Illness in Adults and Children," *Proceedings of the Royal Society of Medicine,* vol. 65, pp. 1035–1040, November 1972.

Holsclaw, Pamela A.: "Nursing in High Emotional Risk Areas," *Nursing Forum,* vol. 4, no. 4, pp. 37–45, 1965.

†Hunt, Gladys M.: *Don't Be Afriad to Die,* Zondervan, Grand Rapids, Michigan, 1971.

Issner, Natalie: "Can the Child Be Distracted from His Disease?" *The Journal of School Health,* vol. 43, no. 7, pp. 468–471, September 1973.

Issner, Natalie: "The Family of the Hospitalized Child," *Nursing Clinics of North America,* vol. 7, no. 1, pp. 5–12, March 1972.

Joling, Robert J.: "The Time of Death," *Arizona Medicine,* pp. 159-163, March 1973.

Kanthor, Harold et al.: "Areas of Responsibility in the Health Care of Multiply Handicapped Children," *Pediatrics,* vol. 54, no. 6, pp. 779–785, December 1974.

†Of interest to parents

Karon, Myron: "The Physician and the Adolescent with Cancer," *Pediatric Clinics of North America*, vol. 20, no. 4, pp. 965–973, November 1973.

Kastenbaum, Robert and Ruth Aisenberg: *The Psychology of Death*, Springer, New York, 1972.

Kavanaugh, Robert E.: *Facing Death*, Penguin, Baltimore, 1972.

Kirkpatrick, J. et al.: "Dilemma of Trust: Relationship Between Medical Care Givers and Parents of Fatally Ill Children," *Pediatrics*, vol. 54, no. 2, pp. 169–175, August 1974.

Kostenbaum, Peter: *Is There an Answer to Death?* Prentice-Hall, Englewood Cliffs, New Jersey, 1976.

Knudson, Alfred G., Jr. and Joseph M. Natterson: "Participation of Parents in the Hospital Care of Fatally Ill Children," *Pediatrics*, vol. 26, no. 3, pp. 482–490, September 1960.

Krakowski, Adam, Jr.: "Doctor-Doctor Relationship III: A Study of Feelings Influencing the Vocation and Its Tasks," *Psychosomatics*, vol. 14, no. 3, pp. 156–161, May-June 1973.

Krant, Melvin J.: *Dying and Dignity: The Meaning and Control of a Personal Death*, Charles C Thomas, Springfield, Ill., 1974.

Krell, Robert: "Problems of the Single Parent Family Unit," *C.M.A. Journal*, vol. 107, pp. 867–872, November 4, 1972.

Kübler-Ross, Elisabeth: *Death: The Final Stage of Growth*, Prentice-Hall, Englewood Cliffs, N. J., 1975.

†Kübler-Ross, Elisabeth: *On Death and Dying*, Macmillan, New York, 1969.

†Kübler-Ross, Elisabeth: *Questions and Answers on Death and Dying*, Macmillan, New York, 1974.

Kübler-Ross, Elisabeth: "What Is It Like to Be Dying?" *American Journal of Nursing*, vol. 71, no. 1, pp. 54–62, January 1971.

Kutscher, Austin H. (ed.): *Death and Bereavement*, Charles C Thomas, Springfield, Ill., 1969.

Lansky, Shirley B. and Grace E. Holmes: "Talking to Parents of an Abnormal Baby," *Continuing Education*, vol. 2, pp. 32–34, May 1974.

Lascari, Andre D. and James A. Stephens: "The Reactions of Families to Childhood Leukemia," *Clinical Pediatrics*, vol. 12, no. 4, pp. 210–214, April 1973.

Lepp, Ignace: *Death and Its Mysteries*, Macmillan, New York, 1968.

Lester, David et al.: "Attitudes of Nursing Students and Nursing Faculty Toward Death," *Nursing Research*, vol. 23, no. 1, pp. 50–53, January-February 1974.

Leyn, Rita M.: "Letters of a Mother in Mourning," *Maternal-Child Nursing Journal*, vol. 4, pp. 83–94, Summer 1975.

Leyn, Rita M.: "A Mother's Reaction to Her Son's Fatal Illness," *Maternal-Child Nursing Journal*, vol. 1, no. 3, pp. 231–241, Fall 1972.

Lifton, Robert Jay and Eric Olson: *Living and Dying*, Bantam, New York, 1974.

Light, Vernon and Richmond, James: "The General Practitioner and the Oncology Organization," *Practitioner*, vol. 210, no. 1260, pp. 748–752, June 1973.

Lukens, John N. and Margaret Miles: "Childhood Leukemia: Meeting the Needs of Patient and Families," *Missouri Medicine*, vol. 67, no. 4, pp. 236–241, April 1970.

†Of interest to parents

MacCarthy, Dermod: "Communication Between Children and Doctor," *Developmental Medicine of Child Neurology,* vol. 16, no. 6, pp. 279–285, December 1974.

McKnew, Donald H., Jr. and Leon Cytryn: "Historical Background in Children with Affective Disorders," *American Journal of Psychiatry,* vol. 130, no. 11, pp. 1278–1280, November 1973.

Maguire, Daniel C.: *Death by Choice,* Doubleday, New York, 1974.

Mann, Sylvia A.: "Coping with a Child's Fatal Illness," *Nursing Clinics of North America,* vol. 9, no. 1, pp. 81–87, March 1974.

Manner, Marya: *Last Rights,* William Morrow, New York, 1974.

Mercer, Ramona T.: "Mothers' Responses to Their Infants with Defects," *Nursing Research,* vol. 23, no. 2, pp. 133–137, March-April 1974.

Miller, Peter G. and Jan Ozga: "Mommy, What Happens When I Die?" *Mental Hygiene,* vol. 57, pp. 20–22, Spring 1973.

Moran, Michael C.: "Grief and Dying," *Hospital Progress,* vol. 55, no. 5, pp. 76–82, May 1974.

†Morris, Jeannie: *Brian Piccolo: A Short Season,* Dell, New York, 1971.

Murstein, Bernard I.: "The Effects of Long-Term Illness of Children on the Emotional Adjustment of Parents," *Child Development,* vol. 31, pp. 157–171, 1960.

Natterson, Joseph M. and Alfred G. Knudson, Jr.: "Observation Concerning Fear of Death in Fatally Ill Children and Their Mothers," *Psychosomatic Medicine,* vol. 22, no. 6, pp. 456–465, November-December 1960.

Parkes, Colin Murray: *Bereavement: Studies of Grief in Adult Life,* International Universities Press, New York, 1972.

Pattison, E. Mansell: *The Experience of Dying,* Prentice-Hall, Englewood Cliffs, N.J., 1977.

Poznanski, Elva Oslow: "The Replacement Child: A Saga of Unresolved Parental Grief," *Journal of Pediatrics,* vol. 81, no. 6, pp. 1190–1193, December 1972.

Reich, Warren T. and Harmon Smith: "The Anguish of Decision—On the Birth of a Severely Handicapped Infant," *Hastings Center Report,* vol. 3, no. 4, pp. 10–12, September 1973.

Richardson, Peggy: "A Multigravida's Use of a Living Child in the Grief and Mourning for a Lost Child," *Maternal-Child Nursing Journal,* vol. 3, no. 3, pp. 181–217, Fall 1974.

†Rogers, Dale Evans: *Angel Unaware,* Fleming H. Revell, Old Tappen, New Jersey, 1953.

Ruitenbeek, Hendrik M. (ed.): *Death Interpretations,* Dell, New York, 1969.

Schnaper, Nathan et al.: *Management of the Dying Patient and His Family,* MSS Information Corporation, New York, 1974.

Schoenberg, Bernard: *Bereavement: Its Psychological Aspects,* Columbia University Press, New York, 1975.

Schoenberg, Bernard et al. (eds.): *Anticipatory Grief,* Columbia University Press, New York, 1974.

Schoenberg, Bernard et al. (eds.): *Psychosocial Aspects of Terminal Care,* Columbia University Press, New York, 1972.

†Of interest to parents

Scofield, Cheryl: "Parents in the Hospital," *Nursing Clinics of North America,* vol. 4, no. 1, pp. 59–67, March 1969.

Smith, Ann G. and Lois T. Schneider: "The Dying Child," *Clinical Pediatrics,* vol. 8, no. 3, pp. 131–134, March 1969.

Solnit, Albert J.: "The Dying Child," *Developmental Medicine of Child Neurology,* vol. 7, pp. 693–704, 1965.

Solnit, Albert J. and Morris Green: "Psychologic Considerations in the Management of Deaths on Pediatric Hospital Service," *Pediatrics,* vol. 24, no. 1, pp. 106–112, July 1959.

Stanko, Barbara: "Crisis Intervention after the Birth of a Defective Child," *The Canadian Nurse,* vol. 69, no. 7, pp. 27–28, July 1973.

Steinfels, Peter and Robert M. Veatch (eds.): *Death Inside Out: The Hastings Center Report,* Harper & Row, New York, 1974–1975.

Strauss, Anselm L. and Barney G. Glaser: *Anguish: A Case History of a Dying Trajectory,* The Sociology Press, Mill Valley, California, 1970.

Sudnow, David: *Passing On: The Social Organization of Dying,* Prentice-Hall, Englewood Cliffs, New Jersey, 1967.

Tew, Brian et al.: "Must a Family with a Handicapped Child Be a Handicapped Family?" *Developmental Medicine and Child Neurology,* vol. 16, Supplement 32, pp. 95–98, 1974.

Tew, Brian and K. M. Laurence: "Mothers, Brothers and Sisters of Patients with Spina Bifida," *Developmental Medicine and Child Neurology,* vol. 15, Supplement 29, pp. 69–76, 1973.

Townes, Brenda D. et al.: "Parental Adjustment to Childhood Leukemia," *Journal of Psychosomatic Research,* vol. 18, no. 1, pp. 9–14, 1974.

Turner, P. J.: "The General Practitioner and the Care of the Dying Patient," *South African Medical Journal,* vol. 48, no. 16, pp. 708–710, April 6, 1974.

Wagner, Bernice M.: "Teaching Students to Work with the Dying," *American Journal of Nursing,* vol. 64, no. 11, pp. 128–131, November 1964.

Watson, M. Jean: "Death—A Necessary Concern for Nurses," *Nursing Outlook,* vol. 16, no. 3, pp. 47–48, February 1968.

Weisman, Avery D.: *On Dying and Denying: A Psychiatric Study of Terminality,* Behavioral Publications, New York, 1972.

Yeaworth, Rosalee C., Frederic T. Kapp, and Carolyn Winget: "Attitudes of Nursing Students Toward the Dying Patient," *Nursing Research,* vol. 23, no. 1, pp. 20–24, January-February 1974.

Young, Janet: "A Mother's Grief Work Following the Death of Her Deformed Child," *Maternal-Child Nursing Journal,* vol. 4, pp. 57–62, Spring 1975.

Sudden Unexpected Death

Beal, Susan: "Sudden Infant Death Syndrome," *The Medical Journal of Australia,* vol. 2, no. 22, pp. 1223–1229, November 25, 1972.

†Beckwith, J. Bruce and Abraham B. Bergman: "SID in Older Infant," National Foundation for Sudden Death, New York, Cat. #004NF.

†Of interest to parents

Bergh, Richard L.: "Let's Talk about Death," *American Journal of Nursing,* vol. 66, no. 1, pp. 71–75, January 1966.

Bergman, Abraham B.: "Psychological Aspects of Sudden Unexpected Death in Infants and Children," *Pediatric Clinics of North America,* vol. 21, no. 1, pp. 115–121, February 1974.

Bergman, Abraham B.: "Sudden Infant Death," *Nursing Outlook,* vol. 20, no. 12, pp. 770–771, December 1972.

Bergman, Abraham B. et al.: "The Psychiatric Toll of the Sudden Infant Death Syndrome," *General Practice,* vol. 40, no. 6, pp. 99–105, December 1969.

†Breches, Edward M.: "Crib Deaths," *Redbook,* July 1968, reprinted by National Foundation for Sudden Infant Death, New York, Cat. #012R-B.

†Burrus, William M.: "The Riddle of Crib Death," *Family Health,* reprinted by National Foundation for Sudden Infant Death, New York, Cat. #013FH.

Byers, Mary Lou: "Crib Death: Foremost Baby Killer Long Ignored by Medical Research," *Science,* vol. 184, pp. 447–449, April 1974.

Byers, Mary Lou: "Play Interviews with a Five Year-Old Boy," *Maternal-Child Nursing Journal,* vol. 1, no. 2, pp. 133–141, Summer 1972.

†Emergy, John L.: "Facts about Sudden Infant Death Syndrome," National Foundation for Sudden Infant Death, New York.

Emergy, John L.: "Welfare of Families of Children Found Unexpectedly Dead ('Cot Deaths')," *British Medical Journal,* vol. 1, no. 5800, pp. 612–615, March 4, 1972.

Friedman, Stanford B.: "Psychological Aspects of Sudden Unexpected Death in Infants and Children," *Pediatric Clinics of North America,* vol. 21, no. 1, pp. 103–111, February 1, 1974.

Green, Morris: "Psychological Aspects of Sudden Unexpected Death in Infants and Children," *Pediatric Clinics of North America,* vol. 21, no. 1, pp. 113–114, February 1974.

Griffin, Jerry J.: "A Crucial Factor in Terminating Life," *American Journal of Nursing,* vol. 75, no. 5, pp. 794–796, May 1975.

Gustafson, James M.: "Mongolism Parental Desires, and the Right to Life," *Perspectives in Biology and Medicine,* vol. 16, no. 4, pp. 529–557, Summer 1973.

Gyulay, Jo-Eileen: "SIDS: Emergency Room Care for Families," *Issues in Comprehensive Pediatric Nursing,* vol. 1, no. 3, pp. 35–47, September-October 1976.

Halpern, Werner I.: "Some Psychiatric Sequelae to Crib Death," *American Journal of Psychiatrics,* vol. 129, no. 4, pp. 58–62, October 1972.

Holder, Angela Roddey: "The Right to Refuse Necessary Treatment," *Law and Medicine,* vol. 221, no. 3, pp. 335–336, July 17, 1972.

Lawler, Mary Kennedy: "Grief Following a Major Accident," *Maternal-Child Nursing Journal,* vol. 1, no. 2, pp. 127–131, Summer 1972.

Morgan, Michael C.: "Grief and Dying," *Hospital Progress,* vol. 55, no. 5, pp. 76, 78, 80, 82, May 1974.

Norman, Margaret G.: "Sudden Infant Death Syndrome," *The Canadian Nurse,* vol. 70, no. 7, pp. 22–23, July 1974.

†Of interest to parents

Patterson, Kathy et al.: "Sudden Infant Death Syndrome," *Nursing '74*, vol. 4, pp. 85–88, May 1974.

Pomeroy, Margaret R.: "Sudden Death Syndrome," *American Journal of Nursing*, vol. 69, no. 9, pp. 1886–1895, September 1969.

Poznanski, Elva Orlow: "The Replacement Child: A Saga of Unresolved Parental Grief," *Behavioral Pediatrics*, vol. 81, no. 6, pp. 1190–1193, December 1972.

Richards, I. D. Gerald and Helen T. McIntosh: "Confidential Inquiry into 226 Consecutive Infant Deaths," *Archives of Disease in Childhood*, vol. 47, pp. 697–706, February 16, 1972.

Salk, Lee: "Sudden Infant Death: Impact on Family and Physician," *Clinical Pediatrics*, vol. 10, no. 5, pp. 248–249, May 1971.

Stitt, Abby: "Emergency after Death," *Emergency Medicine*, vol. 3, no. 3, pp. 270–275, reprinted by National Foundation for Sudden Infant Death, New York, Cat. #100 EM.

Stitt, Abby: "Sudden Infant Death Syndrome (Editorials)," *Postgraduate Medicine*, pp. 156–157, June 1972.

Stitt, Abby: "Sudden Infant Death Syndrome" *Pediatrics*, vol. 50, no. 6, pp. 964–965, December 1972.

Sybist, Carolyn: "The Subsequent Child," National Foundation for Sudden Infant Death, New York.

Tonkie, Shirley: "Sudden Infant Death Syndrome: Hypothesis of Causation," *Pediatrics*, vol. 55, no. 5, pp. 650–660, May 1975.

Trubo, Richard: "Until Crib Death Problem Is Solved, Victims' Parents Need More Help," *Medical News, Journal of the American Medical Association*, vol. 226, no. 11, pp. 1291–1300, December 10, 1973.

Trubo, Richard: "Why Did My Child Die?" *Essence*, February, reprinted by National Foundation for Sudden Infant Death, New York, Cat. #021ES.

†Welch, Wayne: "Why Did My Baby Die?" *Louisville Courier Journal*, August 15, 1971, reprinted by National Foundation for Sudden Infant Death, New York, Cat. #015LC.

Yates, Susan A.: "Stillborn: What a Staff Can Do," *American Journal of Nursing*, vol. 72, no. 3, pp. 1592–1596, September 1972.

Zahourek, Rolhyn and Joseph S. Jensen: "Grieving and the Loss of the Newborn," *American Journal of Nursing*, vol. 73, no. 5, pp. 836–839, May 1973.

PART FOUR

Bennett, M. B.: "Care of the Dying," *South African Medical Journal*, vol. 47, no. 34, pp. 1558–1560, September 1, 1973.

Benoliel, Jeanne Quint: "The Concept of Care for a Child with Leukemia," *Nursing Forum*, vol. 11, no. 2, pp. 194–204, 1972.

Brim, Orville G., Jr. et al. (eds.): *The Dying Patient*, Russell Sage Foundation, New York, 1970.

Denyes, Mary Jean and Anne Altshuler: "Effects of Illness on the Adolescent," in Gladys Scipien et al. (eds.), *Comprehensive Pediatric Nursing*, McGraw-Hill, New York, 1975, pp. 411–422.

†Of interest to parents

Earle, Ann M. et al. (eds.): *The Nurse as Caregiver for the Terminal Patient and His Family,* Columbia University Press, New York, 1976.

Epstein, Charlotte: *Nursing the Dying Patient: Learning Processes for Interaction,* Reston, Va., 1975.

Green, Betty R. and Donald D. Irish (eds.): *Death Education: Preparation for Living,* Schenkman, Cambridge, Mass., 1971.

Hall, Dorothy: "Effects of Illness on the Neonate," in Gladys Scipien et al. (eds.), *Comprehensive Pediatric Nursing,* McGraw-Hill, New York, 1975, pp. 347–353.

Haller, Alex, Jr. et al. (eds.): *The Hospitalized Child and His Family,* The John Hopkins Press, Baltimore, 1967.

Hammar, S. L. and JoAnn Eddy: *Nursing Care of the Adolescent,* Springer, New York, 1966.

Hardgrove, Carol B. and Rosemary B. Dawson: *Parents and Children in the Hospital: The Family's Role in Pediatrics,* Little, Brown, Boston, 1972.

Hobbins, William B.: "What Is a Day of Life Worth?" *R.N.,* vol. 38, no. 4, pp. 33–34, April 1975.

Hopkins, Lois Jones: "A Basis for Nursing Care of the Terminally Ill Child and His Family," *Maternal-Child Nursing Journal,* vol. 2, no. 2, pp. 93–100, Summer 1973.

Jones, Christine H.: "A Kidney Donor: Providing Life after Death," *R.N.,* vol. 38, no. 4, pp. 36–37, April 1975.

Kavanaugh, Robert E.: "Dealing Naturally with the Dying," *Nursing '76,* vol. 6, no. 16, pp. 22–31, October 1976.

Kavanaugh, Robert E.: "Help Patients Who Are Facing Death," *Nursing '74,* vol. 6, no. 6, pp. 35–42, May 1974.

Kneisl, Carol: "Thoughtful Care for the Dying," *American Journal of Nursing,* vol. 68, no. 3, pp. 550–553, March 1968.

Kuhn, Margaret E.: "Death and Dying—The Right to Live—The Right to Die," in *ANA Clinical Sessions 1974,* Appleton-Century-Crofts, New York, 1974.

Lunceford, Janet L.: "Leukemia," *Nursing Clinics of North America,* vol. 2, no. 4, pp. 635–647, December 1967.

Mangen, Sister Frances Xavier: "Psychological Aspects of Nursing: The Advanced Cancer Patient," *Nursing Clinics of North America,* vol. 2, no. 4, pp. 649–658, December 1967.

Martinson, Ida M.: "Why Don't We Let Them Die at Home?" *R.N.,* vol. 39, no. 1, pp. 58–65, January 1976.

Miles, Margaret Shandor and Joyce Olson: "Effects of Illness on the Toddler," in Gladys Scipien et al. (eds.), *Comprehensive Pediatric Nursing,* McGraw-Hill, New York, 1975, pp. 364–375.

Nahigian, Eileen Gallagher: "Effects of Illness on the Preschooler," in Gladys Scipien et al. (eds.), *Comprehensive Pediatric Nursing,* McGraw-Hill, New York, 1975, pp. 376–394.

Noland, Robert L.: *Counseling Parents of the Ill and the Handicapped,* Charles C Thomas, Springfield, Ill., 1971.

Olson, Joyce: "Preparation for Discharge from the Hospital," in Gladys Scipien et al. (eds.), *Comprehensive Pediatric Nursing,* McGraw-Hill, New York, 1975, pp. 453–460.

Olson, Joyce M. and Jo-Eileen Gyulay: "Pediatric Nursing in the Hospital," in Gladys Scipien et al. (eds.), *Comprehensive Pediatric Nursing*, McGraw-Hill, New York, 1975, pp. 901–911.

Petrillo, Madaline and Sirgay Sanger: *Emotional Care of Hospitalized Children*, J. B. Lippincott, Philadelphia, 1972.

Quint, Jeanne: *The Nurse and the Dying Patient*, Macmillan, New York, 1967.

Roberts, Florence Wright: "Effects of Illness on the Infant," in Gladys Scipien et al. (eds.), *Comprehensive Pediatric Nursing*, McGraw-Hill, New York, 1975, pp. 354–363.

Sommer, Carita: "Managing Terminal Care of Herself," *R.N.* vol. 38, no. 4, pp. 37–38, April 1975.

Trufant, Judith A.: "Hospital Admission and Environment," in Gladys Scipien et al. (eds.), *Comprehensive Pediatric Nursing*, McGraw-Hill, New York, 1975, pp. 441–452.

Vernon, David T. A. et al.: *The Psychological Responses of Children to Hospitalization and Illness: A Review of the Literature*, Charles C Thomas, Springfield, Ill., 1965.

Weinberg, Sheila et al.: "Seminars in Nursing Care of the Adolescent," *Nursing Outlook*, vol. 16, no. 12, pp. 18–23, December 1968.

Whisman, Sandra: "Turn the Respirator Off and Let Danny Die," *R.N.*, vol. 38, no. 4, pp. 34–35, April 1975.

Whitman, Helen H. and Shelby J. Lukes: "Behavior Modification for Terminally Ill Patients," *American Journal of Nursing*, vol. 75, no. 1, pp. 98–101, January 1975.

Wiener, Jerry M.: "Response of Medical Personnel to the Fatal Illness of a Child," in Bernard Schoenberg et al. (eds.), *Loss and Grief: Psychological Management in Medical Practice*, Columbia University Press, New York, 1970, pp. 102–118.

Index